At Issue

| Can Diets Be Harmful?

Other Books in the At Issue series:

At Issue

Can Diets Be Harmful?

Ron Lankford, Book Editor

GREENHAVEN PRESS

An imprint of Thomson Gale, a part of The Thomson Corporation

Detroit • New York • San Francisco • New Haven, Conn. • Waterville, Maine • London

Christine Nasso, *Publisher*
Elizabeth Des Chenes, *Managing Editor*

© 2007 Thomson Gale, a part of The Thomson Corporation.

Thomson and Star logo are trademarks and Gale and Greenhaven Press are registered trademarks used herein under license.

For more information, contact:
Greenhaven Press
27500 Drake Rd.
Farmington Hills, MI 48331-3535
Or you can visit our Internet site at http://www.gale.com

LIBRARY OF CONGRESS CATALOGING-IN-PUBLICATION DATA

Can diets be harmful? / Ron Lankford, book editor.
     p. cm. -- (At issue)
   Includes bibliographical references and index.
   ISBN-13: 978-0-7377-3397-6 (hardcover) -- ISBN-13: 978-0-7377-3398-3 (pbk.)
   1. Reducing diets--Health aspects. 2. Diet in disease. I. Lankford, Ronald D., 1962-
   RM222.2.C3668 2007
   613.2'5--dc22
                                                            2007002993

ISBN-10: 0-7377-3397-7 (hardcover)
ISBN-10: 0-7377-3398-5 (pbk.)

Printed in the United States of America
10 9 8 7 6 5 4 3 2 1

Contents

Introduction

With sedentary lifestyles and an abundance of food, many Americans simply take in more calories than they burn, leading to extra weight. This weight gain has been prominent in children and young adults, leading health officials to label the problem an "obesity epidemic." According to Mary G. Harper in *Family and Community Health*, the incidence of overweight children between 6 and 11 has doubled between 1980 and 2000, while the incidence of obesity among young adults between 12 and 19 has tripled. Harper's conclusions are far from isolated. Russell Murdock noted in the periodical *Nation's Health* that 17.1 percent of American children between 2 and 19 were obese, while another 16.5 percent were considered in danger of becoming obese. The Center for Disease Control and Prevention estimates that 9 million young people are overweight. At the current rate, the number of obese children will reach 20 percent in 2010.

The obesity epidemic has health and economic implications, both for the children and young adults who become obese, and for society at large. Obesity has been linked to multiple physical health problems including type 2 diabetes, heart disease, asthma, and sleep disorders. Further, obesity has been linked to mental health disorders including depression and low self-esteem. "The possibility has even been raised," noted the quarterly *Future of Children*, "that given the increasing prevalence of severe childhood obesity, children today may live less healthy and shorter lives than their parents." Health related problems from the obesity epidemic also have economic repercussions. One study estimated that health care costs relating to obesity have risen from $35 million in 1979–1981 to $127 million in 1997–1999.

What Is a Healthy Diet?

In the wake of the obesity epidemic, it has become common for children and adolescents, like adults, to diet. And as with adult diets, young Americans have a staggering number of options, ranging from low-calorie reduction programs to diet camps. While this development has many positive sides, health officials have voiced concern that crash and fad diets may harm the mental and physical development of young adults, and that poor eating habits may lead to eating disorders.

Most nutritionists concur that a healthy weight-loss program is one that provides the body with the essential vitamins and nutrients needed for normal development, and may or may not include a modest calorie reduction. Some argue that by following the United States Department of Agriculture's food pyramid's guidelines for one's age, and reducing unhealthy snacks and soft drinks, many adolescents are able to simply "grow into their weight." For weight reduction, many programs recommend modest calorie reduction with the goal of losing no more than a half or whole pound per week. Simultaneously, young dieters who learn healthier eating habits should be better able to maintain normal weight as adults. It is also essential that anyone wishing to lose weight consult his or her physician or a healthcare official to assure the soundness of individual programs.

Unfortunately, many adolescents who have become obese wish for quicker solutions, and often resort to fad and yo-yo diets. Many fad diets reduce one part of the food pyramid, resulting in low carbohydrate and low protein diets. With low carbohydrate programs, the diet causes a chemical reaction that eliminates water from the body, leading to quick weight loss. When the dieter returns to a normal eating pattern, however, the weight usually returns. Yo-yo diets produce similar problems. When a yo-yo dieter severely restricts his or her calorie intake, the body's metabolism slows down. In effect, a slower metabolism burns fewer calories. When the yo-yo dieter returns to normal eating patterns, the slower metabolism remains, and weight is quickly regained. Both fad diets and yo-yo diets may also cause vitamin and mineral deficiencies, leading to long-term health problems such as weakened bones.

Diet camps, negatively referred to as fat camps, have also become a popular choice for adolescents struggling with obesity. Camps frequently combine two methods to lower an individual's weight: reducing calories and increasing physical activity. Unfortunately, diet camps have sometimes proven ineffective in the long run. Traditionally, camps have placed more emphasis on immediate weight loss than on long-term behavior changes. Some camps include unhealthy, fatty foods in their program, limiting calories by offering smaller servings. Critics fear that without counseling to promote long-term behavior changes and an emphasis on healthier food choices, many children will simply regain the weight once they return from diet camps. "It is easy, after all, to lose weight in a controlled environment," notes Abbey Ellin in the *New York Times,* "but it is a different story when you are back home and faced with temptations like pizza and ice cream and get little to no exercise."

Making Healthy Changes

American adolescents will continue to battle the obesity epidemic with multiple dieting solutions. By making informed decisions, however, young Americans have an opportunity to avoid the health problems associated with obesity and live healthier adult lives. Luckily, the options regarding healthy dieting are becoming easier thanks to initiatives by both health officials and businesses. A number of school lunch programs, long considered a central offender in the obesity epidemic, are challenging the status quo. In one Texas program, each lunch choice must be scanned and matched against an individual student's record; depending on a student's record and the desires of his or her parents, many items are restricted.

Other schools are banning soft drinks and other items from the premises. In a deal brokered by former president William J. Clinton at the end of 2006, companies like Pepsi and Campbell Soup agreed to a number of restrictions regarding food at school. While many critics have called for stricter government regulation, Clinton and the Alliance for a Healthier Generation remained optimistic. "We didn't get in this fix overnight," Clinton was quoted in the *New York Times*, "and we won't get out of it overnight."

Despite positive developments, the obesity epidemic remains a significant social problem and young Americans will continue to rely on dieting to lose extra pounds. The challenge, for parents, health officials, and schools, will be to make sure that young dieters have reliable information to make healthy choices. "Finding a balance between foods that promote health and those that may be less nutritious is important for long term well being," noted Seattle and King County Public Health. Ultimately, the choice—between healthy or unhealthy dieting—will have to be made by children and young adults themselves.

1

Diets Help Support a Healthier Lifestyle

Joan Chamberlain

Joan Chamberlain is a media contact with the National Institute of Diabetes & Digestive & Kidney Diseases.

Marcia Potts, a government employee, had attempted dieting a number of times without success. At 48, she weighed 317 pounds, and was unable to sleep horizontally and plagued by sleep apnea. Finally, she joined a weight-loss program, and while she had few expectations that it would work, she began to lose weight. Potts changed her eating habits, replacing fatty foods with healthier ones, and began walking to the bus stop. At 51, Potts weighs 129 pounds and feels much healthier. Her advice to others who have grown tired of dieting is, "Try one more time."

Nearly 4 years ago, government employee Marcia Potts began changing her life and almost every aspect of her daily habits. Hers is a story of awesome determination and transformation and testimony to the human body's innate ability to recover good health.

Potts had been overweight for most of her adult life, trying and failing on different diets—diet shakes and the cabbage soup diet, among others. "I ate all the time and I ate a lot—probably 3,000 to 5,000 calories a day. I could eat a whole large deep dish pizza by myself. Cheeseburgers were my favorite. Subs. Fries. Lasagna. Things with a lot of cheese. Fattening stuff and lots of it. I ate things 'til they were gone, and they were gone pretty fast."

Joan Chamberlain, "Success Stories," U.S. Department of Health and Human Services, September 2006.

Did she ever feel full? "Never. I still don't."

"Clothes were a problem. Size 28 was too small. I didn't know where to go to buy clothes." She had asthma and sleep apnea, conditions that worsened as she became heavier. She couldn't sleep horizontally, and the apnea awakened her periodically throughout the night. Sleep deprived, she napped through the day. "To walk was unbelievably challenging," she remembers. "I couldn't breathe. I couldn't stand without leaning or holding onto something. The grocery stores were great because I could hang onto a cart." As for seeing a doctor, "I just never went. I knew I'd be told to lose weight. I believed I was going to die from it," she says.

She called her sister, a nurse, to ask for help getting diet pills. Instead, her sister suggested a well-known weight-loss program, which emphasized keeping a journal, cutting fat and calories and reducing portion sizes. On May 23, 2000, Potts joined the program, which met at her work. She remembers the day well. Waiting for the shuttle to go from her office building to the one where the program was held, she had to lean on the mailbox for support. At 48 years old, 5' 3" tall, she weighed 317 pounds. "When I weighed in at 317, my reaction was 'Wow.' In the beginning I had no expectations. I had no idea that I could even get down below 300. I never imagined I would get down to the size I am now. I didn't think I could do it."

Research has shown that a person doesn't need to lose a massive amount of weight to see improvements in health. A modest loss of just 5 to 7 percent of body weight helps a lot.

Making a Healthy Change

"I began by going to the salad bar and filling little containers with healthy foods like lettuce, broccoli, mushrooms, and radishes, and ate that." Gradually, she adjusted to eating lower calorie foods, and her diet became primarily vegetarian. "After a while, I didn't crave anything anymore. It's amazing how your body can adjust."

Potts stuck with the weight-loss program until it ended in August 2000. She lost 163 pounds that year and another 25 pounds the next.

She attributes part of her success to drinking water. "I had no trouble drinking water. Water is my drink. I would drink 32 ounces in the morning, so I'd be sure to get it in." She also began walking. The first day on the program, she walked 20 minutes to the bus stop near her apartment. Slowly, she began adding time and distance to her walks. She began walking the 3/4-mile from her apartment to work and back. She walked regularly at lunch. In the summer, she decided to try the outdoor pool at her apartment building. "On July 13, I swam my first lap." By then she was averaging a loss of 20 pounds a month.

When winter rolled around, she joined a deep-water running class at her local aquatic center. "There I met an instructor, Sally Dimsdale, who became very important to me. She challenged me," recalls Potts. Potts progressed rapidly in that class, and then, with Dimsdale's encouragement, joined other classes in water aerobics and weight training.

"She was always concerned about whether she could handle the next stage," recalls Dimsdale. "She's one of the most disciplined people I know. No excuses. She was single-minded. She truly believed every step she took, every stair she took, and every bite of food—the right kind of food—brought her closer to her goal. She was so motivated."

Potts' message to someone who has given up trying to lose weight? "Try one more time. You can find a way to make it work for you rather than find a way that it won't work for you. And a lot of people do that," she advises. "For example, you have to know what kind of eater you are. I snack. If I get nervous, I eat. But I eat low-calorie foods.

"My energy level is very strong now, and I'm going to need my strength as I get older," says Potts, who at age 51 weighs 129 pounds. "I always want to be under my own control."

Many people don't recognize her anymore. "They probably think I died," she muses.

2

Diets Promote an Unhealthy Lifestyle

Knight-Ridder/Tribune News Service

Knight-Ridder/Tribune News Service offers feature content for newspapers, broadcasters, and the Web.

Fad diets offer the promise of quick weight loss. The loss, however, is often temporary, and the dieter frequently "bounces" back, regaining the lost weight. Quick fix diets, in the form of pills and restrictive eating plans, may also place the dieter's health at risk. Restricting one's diet to certain foods may cause one to lose muscle mass, and if prolonged, may cause heart and kidney damage. Diet pills can also have a number of side effects, including increased blood pressure and rapid heart rate. If a person truly wishes to lose weight, he or she should exercise and reduce calories. To ensure a safe program, individuals should seek the advice of a doctor or dietitian.

Commercial weight-loss plans typically fall into two categories: Those that drastically reduce a person's calorie intake or restrict the dieter to certain foods and those that require a person to take dietary supplements. Dietary supplements are usually pills, but they sometimes include special food bars or drinks.

Most of the popular diets on the market today rely on a person's natural tendency to want to lose weight quickly. They play into a desire for fast results, which is what happened to

Jamie, 16, who followed a 5-day juice diet. Although Jamie lost the weight she wanted, a week later the scale showed she was back to her original weight.

It's quite common for people to quickly gain back all the weight they lose after a few days on a highly restrictive diet. Here's a doctor's answer on why: "The first thing to be aware of with quick weight-loss diets is that our bodies simply aren't designed to drop pounds quickly," says Steven Dowshen, MD, an expert in hormones and the endocrine system. In fact, doctors say that it's nearly impossible for a healthy, normally active teen or adult to lose more than about 3 pounds per week of actual fat from their bodies, even on a starvation diet.

So why does your scale tell you otherwise? "The trick these very low-calorie diets rely on is that your body's natural reaction to near-starvation is to dump water," Dr. Dowshen says. That means that most, if not all, of the weight you lose during the first few days on these diets is water, not fat. You may feel thinner, but you won't look it and you'll probably bounce back up to your original weight once you start eating normally again. "What these diet plans don't tell you is that your body will just suck this lost water back up like a sponge once you start eating more calories again," Dr. Dowshen says.

Sometimes staying on a highly restrictive diet for a long period of time can cause lasting damage to your body, especially to the heart and kidneys.

Losing water weight is also the key to the quick weight-loss claims of some of the diet pills on the market. Many of these pills contain laxatives or diuretics—ingredients that force a person's body to eliminate more water. Other diet pills rely on ingredients that claim to speed up a person's metabolism (the process by which the body turns food into energy and stores unused calories as fat); suppress appetite; or block the absorption of fat, sugars, or carbohydrates.

Do these types of supplements actually do what they say they will? Unfortunately, there's usually no reliable scientific research to back up the claims provided by the product's manufacturer. In addition, there are many unknowns about the substances used in diet supplements, so dietitians and doctors consider them risky. What research studies do show is that most of the people who try one of these "crash" diets regain all the weight they lost within a few weeks or months.

Do These Diets Put Your Health at Risk?

Luckily, very few people stick to a highly restrictive diet for long periods of time and most people give up on them after a few days. But what happens if you keep following extremely low-calorie diets or taking weight-loss supplements? That's when things can get a little scary.

Radically cutting back on calories can make you tired, jittery, and moody. These symptoms usually go away when you resume healthy eating habits, but over the long term, a highly restrictive diet may cause other health problems. You may lose some of your hair, your fingernails may become brittle, dark circles may appear under your eyes, and your muscles may shrink and weaken. Sometimes staying on a highly restrictive diet for a long period of time can cause lasting damage to your body, especially to the heart and kidneys. Following extreme diets over the long term or a pattern of extreme dieting followed by binge eating are both signs that a person may have an eating disorder.

Drastically reducing your food intake depletes the body's access to the vitamins, minerals, and fiber that it needs to stay healthy. If a diet requires you to cut out all dairy products, for example, you are also losing valuable calcium. Over a prolonged period, a lack of calcium puts a person at increased risk for osteoporosis (pronounced: AHS-tee-oh-puh-RO-sis), a condition in which bones become brittle and more susceptible to injury as a person ages. Some diets—like those that omit all red meat—may leave the dieter lacking iron, which can lead to anemia, especially in teen girls. And trying to replace the foods you're cutting out with vitamin pills is a bad idea. Foods like fruits and vegetables contain more than just vitamins and minerals—they are some of the best sources of fiber. Fiber can help to prevent disease.

Restricting food intake over a long period during a person's teenage years can stunt growth. Following restrictive diets over a long period can also delay some of the changes associated with puberty, such as breast development in females and muscle bulk in males. Another side effect of restrictive diets in teenage girls is irregular menstrual periods—or even not getting a period at all.

Another effect of very low-calorie diets is a decrease in resting energy expenditure, or the amount of calories a person burns at rest. One reason for this "slower metabolism" is that people on restrictive diets often lose muscle mass, and muscle burns more calories than fat—even while a person is resting. This makes continuing to lose weight even more difficult and regaining weight easier.

What about the long-term effects of taking diet pills? Common ingredients in diet pills include caffeine, alcohol, 5-hydroxytryptophan (5-HTP), chromium (or chromium picolinate), phentermine, and vanadium. These ingredients may carry health risks for certain people. Ephedrine (also known as ephedra or ma huang), an ingredient in many diet and sports supplements during the late 1990s and early 2000s, was linked to heart problems and may have played a role in the death of at least one professional athlete. The U.S. Food and Drug Administration decided the health risks associated with ephedra were too great, and it banned the substance in December 2003.

If you have any health conditions or are taking medication, always check with your doctor before taking weight-loss supplements because the ingredients in some supplements may interact with specific drugs. For example, 5-HTP may cause adverse reactions in people who take certain medications for depression.

Even ingredients that seem like a normal part of your diet can carry risks when used in weight-loss pills or other stimulants: For example, the average caffeine-based weight-loss pill contains as much caffeine as six cups of coffee. Imagine how wired you'd be if you took two or three of these pills each day! The side effects associated with these products include rapid heart rate, increased blood pressure, dizziness, sleeplessness, seizures, and even addiction.

Furthermore, it's important to know that most diet supplements have not been tested on teen users. Not only does this mean that the dosages prescribed may not be accurate, it could mean that taking certain supplements might carry unknown risks for teens.

If you achieved your weight-loss goal by eating a variety of foods in smaller portions and exercising regularly, chances are better that you will stick with a healthier lifestyle and keep the pounds off in the long run.

Losing Weight for the Long Term

Regardless of concerns about the effectiveness and safety of restrictive diets, keeping the pounds off long term should be the major goal for anyone who wants to lose weight—and that can be more challenging than losing them in the first place. Weight loss is most likely to be successful and lasting when a person changes his or her habits to reduce the overall number of calories he or she eats while at the same time increasing the number of calories burned through exercise. Exercise not only burns calories, it also builds muscle. The more muscle you have, the more efficient your body becomes at burning calories, even when you aren't exercising. You don't have to become a gym rat, though: Walking the family dog, cycling to school, and doing other things that increase your daily level of activity can all make a difference.

Research confirms that one reason people get less exercise these days is because of an increase in "screen time"—in other words, the amount of time spent watching TV, looking at the computer, or playing video games. The American Academy of Pediatrics recommends limiting all screen time to one hour per day. If you're hanging with your friends at the mall instead of chatting to them on the computer, for example, you're getting more exercise.

A survey on health and nutrition conducted by the Centers for Disease Control and Prevention shows that serving sizes for both kids and adults have increased over the past 10 years, and that this is a contributor to obesity. If you super-size your fries or always go for extra hot fudge on your sundae, you are probably taking in more calories than your body can use. Another key dietary factor in weight gain today is the increased consumption of flavored beverages, such as sodas, sweetened juice drinks, and sports drinks. Some people keep a food diary to track what they eat and drink. Writing everything you eat in a daily diary might help you identify those hidden foods that contribute to unwanted weight gain—like the candy bar you usually munch between third and fourth period.

The best way to build a weight-loss program that's right for you is to talk to your doctor or a registered dietitian. During your appointment, your doctor or dietitian may ask you what types of foods you eat, how much weight you want to lose, and the reasons why you want to lose weight. He or she will also help you figure out approximately where your weight should be based on your height and other factors and suggest a sound weight-loss plan that meets your individual needs. (Dietitians report that most guys and girls find weight-loss plans that take their daily schedule and food preferences into account are easier to follow.) The eating plan must include enough calories per day to keep your body working and developing properly. And if you're cutting calories to lose weight, your body will still need to get the same amount of nutrients to stay healthy.

Staying active is an important part of keeping off the weight you've lost. If you achieved your weight-loss goal by eating a variety of foods in smaller portions and exercising regularly, chances are better that you will stick with a healthier lifestyle and keep the pounds off in the long run.

There's a lot of hype out there when it comes to dieting. "Trendy new diets sell books and magazines, so of course you're going to see a lot about the 'hot' new diet of the moment," says Dr. Neil Izenberg, an expert in adolescent medicine and the media. However, "the tried and true approach—cutting back on calories and increasing your level of exercise—is still the best way to lose weight and keep it off," Izenberg says.

3

Diet Misinformation Leads to Unhealthy Choices

National Institute of Diabetes & Digestive & Kidney Diseases

The National Institute of Diabetes & Digestive & Kidney Diseases is part of the U.S. Department of Health and Human Services.

Despite a proliferation of information on dieting, a number of dieting myths persist. Fad diets, for instance, often produce quick weight loss, but are seldom the best way to maintain long-term weight loss. Likewise, diets that promote or limit one part of the food group, or advertise themselves as "natural" or "herbal," may have unintended consequences on individual health. Meal myths, like dieting myths, also persist. Many people believe that they can lose weight by skipping breakfast or eating fewer meals per day, when in truth, those who eat breakfast and four or five meals per day tend to weigh less. The true key to successful weight loss includes exercise and eating reasonably sized portions of a wide variety of healthy foods.

"L*ose 30 pounds in 30 days!*"

"*Eat as much as you want and still lose weight!*"
"*Try the thigh buster and lose inches fast!*"

And so on, and so on. With so many products and weight-loss theories out there, it is easy to get confused.

The information in this fact sheet may help clear up confusion about weight loss, nutrition, and physical activity. It

National Institute of Diabetes & Digestive & Kidney Diseases, "Weight-Loss and Nutrition Myths," http://win.niddk.nih.gov/publications/myths.htm, March 2004.

may also help you make healthy changes in your eating and physical activity habits. If you have questions not answered here, or if you want to lose weight, talk to your health care provider. A registered dietitian or other qualified health professional can give you advice on how to follow a healthy eating plan, lose weight safely, and keep it off.

Diet Myths

Myth: Fad diets work for permanent weight loss.

Fact: Fad diets are not the best way to lose weight and keep it off. Fad diets often promise quick weight loss or tell you to cut certain foods out of your diet. You may lose weight at first on one of these diets. But diets that strictly limit calories or food choices are hard to follow. Most people quickly get tired of them and regain any lost weight.

Fad diets may be unhealthy because they may not provide all of the nutrients your body needs. Also, losing weight at a very rapid rate (more than 3 pounds a week after the first couple of weeks) may increase your risk for developing gallstones (clusters of solid material in the gallbladder that can be painful). Diets that provide less than 800 calories per day also could result in heart rhythm abnormalities, which can be fatal.

> **Tip:** Research suggests that losing 1/2 to 2 pounds a week by making healthy food choices, eating moderate portions, and building physical activity into your daily life is the best way to lose weight and keep it off. By adopting healthy eating and physical activity habits, you may also lower your risk for developing type 2 diabetes, heart disease, and high blood pressure.

Myth: High-protein/low-carbohydrate diets are a healthy way to lose weight.

Fact: The long-term health effects of a high-protein/low-carbohydrate diet are unknown. But getting most of your daily calories from high-protein foods like meat, eggs, and cheese is not a balanced eating plan. You may be eating too much fat and cholesterol, which may raise heart disease risk. You may be eating too few fruits, vegetables, and whole grains, which may lead to constipation due to lack of dietary fiber. Following a high-protein/low-carbohydrate diet may also make you feel nauseous, tired, and weak.

Eating fewer than 130 grams of carbohydrate a day can lead to the buildup of ketones (partially broken-down fats) in your blood. A buildup of ketones in your blood (called ketosis) can cause your body to produce high levels of uric acid, which is a risk factor for gout (a painful swelling of the joints) and kidney stones. Ketosis may be especially risky for pregnant women and people with diabetes or kidney disease.

> **Tip:** High-protein/low-carbohydrate diets are often low in calories because food choices are strictly limited, so they may cause short-term weight loss. But a reduced-calorie eating plan that includes recommended amounts of carbohydrate, protein, and fat will also allow you to lose weight. By following a balanced eating plan, you will not have to stop eating whole classes of foods, such as whole grains, fruits, and vegetables—and miss the key nutrients they contain. You may also find it easier to stick with a diet or eating plan that includes a greater variety of foods.

Myth: Starches are fattening and should be limited when trying to lose weight.

Fact: Many foods high in starch, like bread, rice, pasta, cereals, beans, fruits, and some vegetables (like potatoes and yams) are low in fat and calories. They become high in fat and calories when eaten in large portion sizes or when covered with high-fat toppings like butter, sour cream, or mayonnaise. Foods high in starch (also called complex carbohydrates) are an important source of energy for your body.

Tip: A healthy eating plan is one that:

- Emphasizes fruits, vegetables, whole grains, and fat-free or low-fat milk and milk products.

- Includes lean meats, poultry, fish, beans, eggs, and nuts.

- Is low in saturated fats, trans fat, cholesterol, salt (sodium), and added sugars.

Myth: Certain foods, like grapefruit, celery, or cabbage soup, can burn fat and make you lose weight.

Fact: No foods can burn fat. Some foods with caffeine may speed up your metabolism (the way your body uses energy, or calories) for a short time, but they do not cause weight loss.

> **Tip:** The best way to lose weight is to cut back on the number of calories you eat and be more physically active.

Myth: Natural or herbal weight-loss products are safe and effective.

Fact: A weight-loss product that claims to be "natural" or "herbal" is not necessarily safe. These products are not usually scientifically tested to prove that they are safe or that they work. For example, herbal products containing ephedra (now banned by the U.S. Government) have caused serious health problems and even death. Newer products that claim to be ephedra-free are not necessarily danger-free, because they may contain ingredients similar to ephedra.

> **Tip:** Talk with your health care provider before using any weight-loss product. Some natural or herbal weight-loss products can be harmful.

Meal Myths

Myth: "I can lose weight while eating whatever I want."

Fact: To lose weight, you need to use more calories than you eat. It is possible to eat any kind of food you want and lose weight. You need to limit the number of calories you eat every day and/or increase your daily physical activity. Portion control is the key. Try eating smaller amounts of food and choosing foods that are low in calories.

Tip: When trying to lose weight, you can still eat your favorite foods—as long as you pay attention to the **total number of calories** that you eat.

Myth: Low-fat or fat-free means no calories.

Fact: A low-fat or fat-free food *is* often lower in calories than the same size portion of the full-fat product. But many processed low-fat or fat-free foods have just as many calories as the full-fat version of the same food—or even more calories. They may contain added sugar, flour, or starch thickeners to improve flavor and texture after fat is removed. These ingredients add calories.

Tip: Read the Nutrition Facts on a food package to find out how many calories are in a serving. Check the serving size too—it may be less than you are used to eating. For more information about reading food labels, visit the U.S. Food and Drug Administration online at www.cfsan.fda.gov/˜dms/foodlab.html.

Myth: Fast foods are always an unhealthy choice and you should not eat them when dieting.

Fact: Fast foods can be part of a healthy weight-loss program with a little bit of know-how.

Tip: Avoid supersize combo meals, or split one with a friend. Sip on water or fat-free milk instead of soda. Choose salads and grilled foods, like a grilled chicken breast sandwich or small hamburger. Try a "fresco" taco (with salsa instead of cheese or sauce) at taco stands. Fried foods, like french fries and fried chicken, are high in fat and calories, so order them only once in a while, order a small portion, or split an order with a friend. Also, use only small amounts of high-fat, high-calorie toppings, like regular mayonnaise, salad dressings, bacon, and cheese.

Myth: Skipping meals is a good way to lose weight.

Fact: Studies show that people who skip breakfast and eat fewer times during the day tend to be heavier than people who eat a healthy breakfast and eat four or five times a day. This may be because people who skip meals tend to feel hungrier later on, and eat more than they normally would. It may also be that eating many small meals throughout the day helps people control their appetites.

> **Tip:** Eat small meals throughout the day that include a variety of healthy, low-fat, low-calorie foods. For more information about healthy eating, read the Weight-control Information Network brochure *Healthy Eating and Physical Activity Across Your Lifespan: Tips for Adults.*

Myth: Eating after 8 p.m. causes weight gain.

Fact: It does not matter what time of day you eat. It is what and how much you eat and how much physical activity you do during the whole day that determines whether you gain, lose, or maintain your weight. No matter when you eat, your body will store extra calories as fat.

> **Tip:** If you want to have a snack before bedtime, think first about how many calories you have eaten that day. And try to avoid snacking in front of the TV at night—it may be easier to overeat when you are distracted by the television.

Physical Activity Myth

Myth: Lifting weights is not good to do if you want to lose weight, because it will make you "bulk up."

Fact: Lifting weights or doing strengthening activities like push-ups and crunches on a regular basis can actually help you maintain or lose weight. These activities can help you build muscle, and muscle burns more calories than body fat. So if you have more muscle, you burn more calories—even sitting still. Doing strengthening activities 2 or 3 days a week will not "bulk you up." Only intense strength training, combined with a certain genetic background, can build very large muscles.

> **Tip:** In addition to doing at least 30 minutes of moderate-intensity physical activity (like walking 2 miles in 30 minutes) on most days of the week, try to do strengthening activities 2 to 3 days a week. You can lift weights, use large rubber bands (resistance bands), do push-ups or sit-ups, or do household or garden tasks that make you lift or dig.

Food Myths

Myth: Nuts are fattening and you should not eat them if you want to lose weight.

Fact: In small amounts, nuts can be part of a healthy weight-loss program. Nuts are high in calories and fat. However, most nuts contain healthy fats that do not clog arteries. Nuts are also good sources of protein, dietary fiber, and minerals including magnesium and copper.

> **Tip:** Enjoy small portions of nuts. One-half ounce cup of nuts has about 270 calories.

Myth: Eating red meat is bad for your health and makes it harder to lose weight.

Fact: Eating lean meat in small amounts can be part of a healthy weight-loss plan. Red meat, pork, chicken, and fish contain some cholesterol and saturated fat (the least healthy kind of fat). They also contain healthy nutrients like protein, iron, and zinc.

> **Tip:** Choose cuts of meat that are lower in fat and trim all visible fat. Lower fat meats include pork tenderloin and beef round steak, tenderloin, sirloin tip, flank steak, and extra lean ground beef. Also, pay attention to portion size. Three ounces of meat or poultry is the size of a deck of cards.

Myth: Dairy products are fattening and unhealthy.

Fact: Low-fat and fat-free milk, yogurt, and cheese are just as nutritious as whole-milk dairy products, but they are lower in fat and calories. Dairy products have many nutrients your body needs. They offer protein to build muscles and help organs work properly, and calcium to strengthen bones. Most milks and some yogurts are fortified with vitamin D to help your body use calcium.

> **Tip:** The 2005 *Dietary Guidelines for Americans* recommends consuming 3 cups per day of fat-free/low-fat milk or equivalent milk products. For more information on these guidelines, visit www.healthierus.gov/dietaryguidelines.

> If you cannot digest lactose (the sugar found in dairy products), choose low-lactose or lactose-free dairy products, or other foods and beverages that offer calcium and vitamin D (listed below).

> **Calcium:** soy-based beverage or tofu made with calcium sulfate; canned salmon; dark leafy greens like collards or kale

> **Vitamin D:** soy-based beverage or cereal (getting some sunlight on your skin also gives you a small amount of vitamin D)

Myth: "Going vegetarian" means you are sure to lose weight and be healthier.

Fact: Research shows that people who follow a vegetarian eating plan, on average, eat fewer calories and less fat than nonvegetarians. They also tend to have lower body weights relative to their heights than nonvegetarians. Choosing a vegetarian eating plan with a low fat content may be helpful for weight loss. But vegetarians—like nonvegetarians—can make food choices that contribute to weight gain, like eating large amounts of high-fat, high-calorie foods or foods with little or no nutritional value.

Vegetarian diets should be as carefully planned as nonvegetarian diets to make sure they are balanced. Nutrients that nonvegetarians normally get from animal products, but that are not always found in a vegetarian eating plan, are iron, calcium, vitamin D, vitamin B12, zinc, and protein.

> **Tip:** Choose a vegetarian eating plan that is low in fat and that provides all of the nutrients your body needs. Food and beverage sources of nutrients that may be lacking in a vegetarian diet are listed below.
>
> **Iron:** cashews, spinach, lentils, garbanzo beans, fortified bread or cereal
>
> **Calcium:** dairy products, fortified soy-based beverages, tofu made with calcium sulfate, collard greens, kale, broccoli
>
> **Vitamin D:** fortified foods and beverages including milk, soy-based beverages, or cereal
>
> **Vitamin B12:** eggs, dairy products, fortified cereal or soy-based beverages, tempeh, miso (tempeh and miso are foods made from soybeans)
>
> **Zinc:** whole grains (especially the germ and bran of the grain), nuts, tofu, leafy vegetables (spinach, cabbage, lettuce)
>
> **Protein:** eggs, dairy products, beans, peas, nuts, seeds, tofu, tempeh, soy-based burgers

4

Diet Obsession Stems from Sedentary Lifestyles

Michael Jay Friedman

Michael Jay Friedman is a program officer in the Bureau of Information Programs at the Department of State.

Over the expanse of history, the human body learned to store fat cells for times of scarcity. Because of modern agriculture, however, Americans now live in a land of abundance. This abundance of food, combined with sedentary lifestyles, has led to widespread obesity in recent years. Americans frequent fast-food restaurants and have replaced home-cooked meals with processed foods. Americans also spend more time in front of the television and computers, and participate in fewer physical activities like walking. As a result, obesity has increased 74 percent since 1991, and Americans have become obsessed with dieting.

Americans are blessed with an unprecedented abundance and variety of food. Surrounded by convenient, appealing, and affordable meals, often high in calories, many Americans overindulge. A lifestyle of eating more and exercising less has led to a sharp rise in obesity. The health consequences are profound, and the social burdens substantial. Increasing numbers of Americans are recognizing that plentiful food requires intelligent choices.

For most of their six million years, human beings were hunter-gatherers who hunted, fished, and foraged for their food. Since the source of one's next meal could be highly un-

Michael Jay Friedman, "The Fat of the Land: America Confronts Its Weight Problem," *U.S. Society & Values*, July 2004, pp. 35–37.

certain, Homo sapiens evolved to survive a scarcity of food. Our bodies store excess calories as fat, and then convert that fat into energy when food is unavailable. This finely tuned metabolic system serves us well, but it is not designed to process steady overeating. Simply put, the body will continue to store surplus energy as fat, even when the resulting extra weight is harmful.

Lifestyle Changes

Modern agriculture ended food scarcity in America, but only in the past few years have diet and lifestyle changes produced widespread obesity. One change is that Americans consume more processed foods. These can be both tasty and convenient, and they typically are cheaper per calorie than whole fruits and vegetables. But processing often adds flavoring ingredients like sugar (11 percent of U.S. caloric intake in 1970, 16 percent today), oils, and starches.

Another change is that Americans are more likely to eat at restaurants, and especially at fast food restaurants. Americans "eat out" twice as often today as they did in 1970, spending more than 40 cents of every food dollar at restaurants. We have become especially partial to fast food. Sales have increased 200 percent over the past 20 years, to the point where one American in four eats in a fast food establishment on any given day. With the cost-per-calorie so low, Americans have grown accustomed to larger portions: on average, today's hamburgers are 23 percent and soft drink servings 52 percent larger than they were 20 years ago.

Changes in diet are related to changes in lifestyle. Americans often live alone, or in families where both husband and wife work. With less time available for meal planning and food preparation, processed foods provide attractive alternatives. A microwave oven can heat a frozen meal in minutes. Fast food restaurants feature "drive-thru" windows where a parent returning home from work can purchase dinner for a hungry family without even leaving his or her car! These meals may feature more "empty calories" (those devoid of nutrients) than a traditional home-cooked meal, but for time-pressed Americans, the tradeoff is often acceptable.

The number of overweight or obese Americans has increased by 74 percent since 1991.

Other lifestyle changes affect the second half of the obesity equation—exercise. Physically active people burn off the calories they consume. However, Americans increasingly live in communities where both shopping and work are inaccessible except by car or public transportation. In the past 25 years, travel by foot and bicycle has declined by 40 percent. Meanwhile, the nature of work has changed. Fewer Americans engage in strenuous industrial activity. Instead, they are often sitting before a computer screen manipulating data. At home, pastimes such as television viewing and Internet surfing contribute to the general decline in physical activity, making it all the harder to shed calories and pounds. Tellingly, obesity is less of a problem in New York City, where travel by foot—to work, shopping, and entertainment—is more common than in almost all other U.S. communities.

Waistline Expansion

The result has been a rapid and unhealthy expansion of the American waistline. The number of overweight or obese Americans has increased by 74 percent since 1991. Fully two-thirds of adult Americans fall into one of these categories. (The National Centers for Chronic Disease Prevention and Health Promotion in Atlanta, Georgia, has developed a formula—known as the body mass index, or BMI—for calculating body fat in relation to lean body mass. Anyone with a BMI of 25 to 29.9 is considered to be overweight, and anyone with a BMI of 30 or above is considered to be obese.)

The health consequences have been profound. Medical treatments of resulting health problems now cost in excess of one hundred million ($100,000,000) dollars annually. It is estimated that at least 300,000 Americans die each year from obesity-related conditions like diabetes and heart disease; obesity may now be the leading contributor to premature death among Americans. Serious as these statistics are, they do not depict how excess weight can deprive one of the ability to engage in and enjoy a variety of activities common in everyday life.

Widespread obesity is a recent phenomenon, but many Americans now recognize the importance of careful attention to diet and lifestyle. Consumers pay some $34 million on diet products each year. Their results vary, as proper weight control typically requires healthful habits rather than a "quick fix." Encouraging signs include the introduction of healthier yet equally convenient snack foods and greater availability of diet-friendly entrees. Even the fast food industry reports a 16 percent increase in sales of main-dish salads over the past year. To shed weight and remain healthy, individuals will have to consider carefully what they eat and how they go about their daily routines. Increasingly, Americans are learning that they cannot indulge without limits in what can seem to be an unlimited bounty. Among positive steps that Americans are taking in this direction are better food labeling, more nutritious and better-balanced school lunches, public awareness campaigns, and greater availability of low-calorie options at restaurants.

Diets: A Bewildering Variety

Americans are seemingly obsessed with dieting, and their reasons for following a specific diet vary widely.

Most dieters are motivated by a desire to lose weight and, in so doing, to improve their health and appearance, but there are many other reasons. Among them are religious beliefs that proscribe certain foods; ethical rationales, such as an aversion to killing animals, a common motivation for vegetarianism; a desire to help preserve the environment by avoiding certain foods whose production is perceived as environmentally destructive, or as part of a broader philosophy of life.

An amazing variety of diets are available in books, in magazines, and on the Internet. They vary widely in terms of the foods they prescribe or forbid; the emphases they place on such things as calories, fats, carbohydrates, and exercise; and on their methodologies.

This plethora of choices ensures that if one diet fails to bring about the desired result, there is always another that can be tried. Here are some of the most popular diets that Americans are following today:

Atkins Diet

- Popularized by the late cardiologist Dr. Robert Atkins

- Severely restricts refined carbohydrates, such as sugar and white flour

- Allows a wide variety of other foods, such as meat

- Few restrictions on fat or calories

- Has four phases: Induction, Ongoing Weight Loss, Pre-Maintenance, and Lifetime Maintenance

Beverly Hills Diet

- Popularized by Judy Mazel, dietician and author

- Recommends eating fruit by itself

- Prohibits protein being eaten with carbohydrates

- Begins with a 35-day plan that gives specific items to be eaten at each meal

Scarsdale Diet

- Popularized by the late cardiologist Dr. Herman Tarnower

- Sets forth a seven to 14-day plan

- Outlines types of foods that can and cannot be eaten

- Emphasizes fruits, vegetables, and lean sources of protein

- Snacking forbidden

South Beach Diet

- Popularized by cardiologist Dr. Arthur Agatston

- Organized in three phases

- Allows normal portions of lean proteins like fish and chicken

- Forbids the intake of bread, rice, pasta, sugar, or baked goods in Phase 1, which lasts 14 days

- Allows unlimited amounts of certain vegetables but not high glycemic ones like beets, carrots, corn, and sweet potatoes

Weight Watchers ™

- Emphasizes a comprehensive lifestyle program including regular meetings in which dieters encourage each other

- Emphasizes lifestyle changes; for example, activities to reduce boredom eating

- All foods are assigned a point value based on fat, fiber, and calorie content

- No list of forbidden foods, but maximum point values should not be exceeded

Fit For Life

- Popularized by nutritionist Harvey Diamond

- Relies heavily on fruits and vegetables

- Severely restricts dairy products and meats

- Attempts to teach dieters to eat in accordance with what are described as "natural digestive cycles"

Vegan Diet

- Strict vegetarian diet that proscribes meat and all other animal products, including cheese and milk

5

Fad Diets Promote Unhealthy Eating Habits

Camilla Wells

Camilla Wells is a writer for Iris: A Journal About Women.

At any given time, 50 percent of American women are dieting, and millions suffer from eating disorders. Unsatisfied with their body image, women frequently embrace fad diets in an effort to lose weight quickly. If followed over a long period of time, however, fad diets can be unhealthy, raising the risks of skin cancer, heart disease, and diabetes. Unfortunately, the perceived need to lose weight becomes an obsession, leading to continual dieting and unhealthy eating patterns.

Ever wonder how the American diet industry manages to rake in more than $40 billion a year? Considering that 5 million American women suffer from full-blown eating disorders such as bulimia and anorexia, "80 percent of women have been on a diet, half are actively dieting at any given time, and half report feeling dissatisfied with their bodies all the time" the immense profitability of the diet industry begins to make sense. Half of all American women monitor their eating habits on a day-to-day basis. Half of American women—consciously or unconsciously—are attempting to fit a near-impossible mold established by wispy-thin celebrities.

This widespread need to diet is known as a woman's "normative obsession" (a phrase coined by psychologist Judith Rodin, president of the University of Pennsylvania). This normative obsession manifests itself as the recurring comparison to other women and their bodies, guilt over simple indulgences in eating, and the ascetic monitoring of diet. Such monitoring takes place on a daily basis, and often occurs in women who wish to control their weight so that they can maintain what they feel is a "normal" attractive appearance. Though not technically a severe eating disorder, such tight control over weight gain and loss can wear on a woman's wellbeing. This obsession can become so strong that it is, as Joan Blumberg says, an "emotional addiction."

The Dangers of Fad Diets

This normative obsession often manifests itself in the form of fad diets. Now, more than before, it seems that we cannot turn anywhere without seeing advertisements for "low-carb" foods, which are the staples of such regimens as the Zone, the South Beach, and the Atkins diets. Some stores even advertise plain cheese and eggs as "low-carb" foods. Low-carb is the "diet poison" of the moment, allowing millions of men and women to quickly lose 20, 30, or even 60 pounds. These diets are a quick fix for the flabby tummies and thighs of Americans, which is probably why an estimated 17.2 percent of the country is counting their carbs. By making the body go into ketosis, a type of starvation mode, one is able to lose weight rapidly. "The body, overloading on fat and protein, theoretically breaks down fat cells for energy and sheds pounds of water as it struggles to get rid of toxic breakdown products." But toxins and pounds aren't the only casualties of Atkins.

To stay thin, dieters often neglect nutritional balance, sticking to a diet that isn't healthy for them in the long run. Indeed, the Atkins Diet, as well as other low-carb diets, may have disastrous consequences in addition to its immediate benefits. The American Heart association explains its possible side effects: "Eating large amounts of high-fat foods for a sustained period raises the risk of coronary heart disease, diabetes, stroke and several types of cancer. People who can't use excess protein effectively may be at higher risk of kidney and liver disorders, and osteoporosis." And according to Dr. Paul Robinson, who treated Rachel Huskey (a 16-year-old girl purported to have died due to heart arrhythmia caused by a low-carb diet), dieters shed calcium and potassium along with the pounds, which robs them of electrolytes essential for maintaining a regular heartbeat.

Unhealthy Eating Patterns

Why would such a seemingly unhealthy diet have such mass appeal? Well, Atkins has fast results and is relatively easy to follow, particularly in the first couple of months. There are no limits on the fats and proteins that you may eat, so you can gorge yourself on bunless hamburgers, cheesy omelets, and mountains of mayonnaise. This diet, at least temporarily, fills you up with some of your favorite fats.

But it is my belief that these diets encourage an unhealthy pattern of eating for many people, particularly women. The effects of these diets are not intrinsically permanent. When a woman attempts to go off such a diet, she is often met with disaster—for the key to keeping the pounds off on the Atkins diet is the maintenance of a low-carb count. Any reintroduction of carbs and your body slips out of starvation mode and into the mode of weight gain. In this way, these fad diets encourage normative obsession: in order to lose weight and keep it off—and thus stay "normal"—one's diet must be consistently monitored and restricted, allowing for very little inattention.

6

Sticking with One Diet Improves Health

Rosalie Marion Bliss

Rosalie Marion Bliss is a public affairs specialist with the Agricultural Research Service.

Research shows that sticking with one diet, regardless of the type, is more important than the diet one chooses. What matters most is that individuals lose more weight by remaining with the same diet over a long period of time. Because of this, it is important to choose a diet that does not conflict with an individual's typical food choices. Sticking with the same diet for a year will also improve good-to-bad cholesterol rates and lower blood insulin levels.

With over 1,000 diet books available on bookstore shelves, popular diets clearly have become increasingly prevalent. At the same time, they have also become increasingly controversial, because some depart substantially from mainstream medical advice or have been criticized by various medical authorities.

A comparison of several popular diets by *ARS* [Agricultural Research Service]-funded researchers showed that at the end of the day, or in this case at the end of the year, sticking with a diet—more than the type of a diet—is the key to losing weight.

The study was conducted by Michael L. Dansinger, Ernst J. Schaefer, and Joi A. Gleason of the Lipid Metabolism Labora-

Rosalie Marion Bliss, "A 'Stick-To-It' Diet Is More Important than a Popular One," *Agricultural Research*, vol. 54, March 2006, p. 19.

tory at the Jean Mayer USDA Human Nutrition Research Center on Aging at Tufts University and Tufts-New England Medical Center in Boston.

Published last year in the *Journal of the American Medical Association*, the study compared the relative merits of four of the most popular weight-loss diets. These included the Atkins (carbohydrate restriction), Ornish (fat restriction), Weight Watchers (calorie and portion size restriction), and Zone (high-glycemic-load carbohydrate restriction and increased protein) diets.

Sticking with One Diet

The researchers randomly assigned 160 overweight or obese volunteers to use 1 of the 4 diets. All participants were provided with the diet book and four 1-hour instructional classes to help them assimilate the rules of their assigned diets. The 40 participants in each of the 4 diet groups were representative—in terms of age, race, sex, body mass index, and metabolic characteristics—of the overweight population in the United States.

The results in terms of both weight loss and reduction in heart disease risk factors were compared among "completers," or those who stayed with the study for an entire year.

Only about half the volunteers completed the program while on what the authors considered to be more extreme diet plans: Atkins and Ornish diets. In contrast, 65 percent were able to complete the more moderate diet plans: Weight Watchers and Zone. Still, those that stayed in the program tended to loosen their resolve by about 6 months, as determined by their self-reported food records.

"The bottom line was that it wasn't so much the type of diet followed that led to successful weight loss, but the ability of participants to stick with the program for the entire year's time," says Schaefer.

"The study showed that whether volunteers restricted carbohydrate calories or fat calories—whether they lowered intake overall, or balanced intake overall—everybody lost weight," says Schaefer. "Ultimately, it comes down to calorie restriction. The strongest predictor of weight loss was not the type of diet, but compliance with the diet plan that subjects were given."

The finding lends credence to the importance of adopting a caloric-restriction diet that doesn't conflict with one's natural affinities for specific allowable foods.

"Implementing a dietary regimen that can transition an individual into a healthful eating pattern after the diet ends is also very important," says ARS Human Nutrition National Program Leader Molly Kretsch. "Lifestyle practices that help people maintain a healthy body weight, incorporate the right balance of foods and appropriate portion sizes, and increase their physical activity are the keys to long-term weight management."

Healthy Results

Among those who stayed in the program for the entire 12-month period, all four diet plans promoted a 10-percent improvement in the balance of "good" (HDL) and "bad" (LDL) cholesterol levels. "The particular diet plan the long-term dieter followed did not seem to matter that much," says Dansinger. "The long-term dieters reduced their ratio of good to bad cholesterol according to how much weight they lost."

Those who improved their cholesterol ratios by 10 percent improved their heart disease risk factors by 20 percent. "For every 1 percent of weight loss a dieter achieves, there will be a 2-percent, or twice as much, reduction in heart disease risk factors," says Dansinger.

In addition, all four diet plans promoted lower blood insulin levels as well as lower levels of C reactive protein (CRP). High levels of CRP in the blood have been linked to heart disease.

Future studies will focus on identifying practical techniques to increase dietary adherence—including ways to match individuals with the diets best suited to their food preferences and lifestyles. "We also plan to test different versions of the new USDA diet and look specifically at the results from a diet with higher and lower glycemic index values," says Schaefer.

7

Fast Food Can Be Part of a Healthy Diet

Suzanne S. Brown

Suzanne S. Brown is a staff writer for the Denver Post.

While fast food has received a bad rap for being high in calories and fat content, it is possible to eat healthy at popular restaurant chains. A great deal of information describing calories and fat content is available in brochures and online. It is possible to eat healthier at fast-food restaurants by eating smaller portions and by cutting back on items with high fat content. There are also more healthy choices for children at these restaurants today. By carefully researching menus, eating out infrequently, and by using common sense, it is possible to eat at fast-food chains without increasing one's waistline or cholesterol level.

Fast food is easy to criticize but hard to avoid. Most people who are truthful will admit to eating it, even if only occasionally.

Take Mary Lee Chin, a registered dietitian and spokeswoman for the Colorado Dietetic Association. She recently went on a road trip with her son and ended up in many a drive-through lane wondering how to pick something nutritious and non-fattening on the menu.

"If only I would've done this research before I left," she said after studying the menus and nutritional data on dozens of items available at a handful of popular fast-food restaurants.

We enlisted Chin to help us find out if it's possible to feed yourself and your children a healthy meal on the go. The good news is yes, but you'll need to rethink your approach and do some research.

As bad a rap as they get, fast-food restaurants are serving healthier options and offering abundant nutritional data in brochures and online. Who knew you could get a salad with edamame and snow peas at McDonald's? Or one with crisp apples, cranberries and walnuts at Arby's? How about a veggie burger at the bastion of big meat, Burger King? Even Taco Bell is offering popular items "Fresco" style, with salsa subbing for sauce or cheese.

Granted, the word might be spreading a little slowly. Only one other customer besides Chin was sampling an Asian salad with grilled chicken at the McDonald's she visited on a recent lunch hour. And it can be confusing sorting out calorie and fat content, as well as downright scary reading the sodium statistics on many items.

Chin helped us develop a number of guidelines for selecting fast food.

Fast Food Menus Online

Do your homework: how much better for you is a grilled chicken sandwich than a double cheeseburger? Restaurant websites have become a helpful source of information, offering not only nutritional content, but calculators that let you place items on your hypothetical "tray" so you can take a look at the numbers. McDonald's and Taco Bell's sites are two of the best, offering not just raw data, but percentages of the "Daily Values" (DVs) of nutrients that have a significant impact on health and fitness.

Chin is a big fan of having DVs listed on menus for such items as fat, saturated fat, cholesterol and sodium. For example, the Daily Value for fat, based on a 2,000-calorie diet, is

65 grams. So if you eat a Quarter Pounder with cheese and large fries, you're consuming 55 grams of fat, almost an entire day's worth.

Many restaurants detail ingredients on every item they offer, including condiments, and list allergens as well.

"DVs are not recommended intakes on amounts of nutrients to eat every single day. They're reference points," Chin says.

The dietitian recommends going online to look at menus and making notes on items that will be healthy choices when you find yourself in the drive-through lane. Write the information on index cards or sticky notes and leave them in your car.

Also be alert to new items on menus, particularly those featuring chicken or fish, fresh fruit, yogurt, whole-wheat bread and tortillas, salads with dressing on the side (and fat-free dressings), fat-free or low-fat milk and bottled water.

Many restaurants detail ingredients on every item they offer, including condiments, and list allergens as well. (Quizno's was the only big chain restaurant we found that didn't list full nutritionals on its website, giving content for only two sandwiches and some low-carbohydrate options, and requesting visitors send an e-mail for nutrition information.)

Size matters: Downsize rather than supersize your meal and you'll do your waistline a favor. Triple-meat burgers and French-fry portions that could feed a family of four are now offered to single diners. Bagels today are twice the size they were 20 years ago, Chin says. Scale back on the size of the portions you order and you'll reduce the amount of calories, fat and other undesirable ingredients.

Hold the mayo, hold the dressing: It might take a minute longer to get your meal, but if you ask that mayonnaise, cheese and various dressings be left off your sandwich, you'll enjoy a leaner, healthier lunch. Fast-food restaurants typically offer the dressing for salads in separate packets, as they also do with nuts and other add-ons.

Healthy Choices

Visit restaurants like Wendy's and McDonald's where you can get a side salad or fruit salad rather than fries to reduce a meal's calories and fat.

Eat your greens: The smell of grilled burgers is inviting, but salads are the nutritional stars in fast-food restaurants. If you order one with chicken and refrain from too many add-ons, you can get a meal with decent protein and vegetable content. Just don't expect heaping portions of the good stuff—the snow peas, red peppers and edamame were meagerly distributed in our salad from McDonald's.

Salad dressings can add 200 calories and 18 grams of fat (McDonald's Caesar, for example), but we found using only half the amount in the packet amply dressed our greens.

Also ask about getting an entree prepared as a salad. Subway offers its sandwich ingredients served over a bed of spinach or lettuce, for example. Order the fat-free Italian dressing (35 calories, no fat) rather than the Atkins honey mustard (200 calories, 22 grams of fat).

Make good choices for kids: Not too long ago, children's fast food meals consisted of a sandwich, fries and a soft drink. Now parents often have a choice of such side items as a fruit cup, yogurt, applesauce, milk or juice, all items that will raise the nutritional value of a meal and still please young taste buds.

Chin suggests paying attention to fat calories in children's meals, as they should be less than 30 percent of the total calories. That figure is easy to surpass at such restaurants as Taco Bell, where a recommended child's meal is two tacos and an order of cinnamon twists, which make up 39 percent of the total fat and 47 percent of the saturated fat a person should have in a day. "You'll need to make very careful choices the rest of the day," she says.

Using Common Sense

Pass on the salt: The levels of sodium in many fast-food items is dangerously high and should be reason enough to keep you from making a habit of eating this type of meal, Chin says.

For example, the Daily Value for sodium is 2,300 milligrams a day. A Burger King Whopper with cheese and a large order of fries have 2,270mg sodium, a shake short of a day's worth in a single meal.

On average, the higher a person's salt intake, the higher his blood pressure. "Keeping blood pressure in the normal range reduces a person's risk of coronary disease, stroke, congestive heart failure and kidney disease," Chin says.

Liquid diets: It is tempting and delicious to drink your meal at a place like Jamba Juice rather than eating it at a restaurant, but the dietitian offers some cautions.

First, take a hard look at calories and portion control. The "power" size of a Razzmatazz smoothie at Jamba Juice contains 620 calories, almost a third of the 2,000-calorie diet recommended for many adult women. In addition, if you're worried about calories, watch out for smoothies made with frozen yogurt and sherbet bases.

Also, "Health claims for power, energy, and immune-system boosts have not been evaluated by the FDA," Chin says. "While research on supplemental ingredients has been promising, it is still way too early" to know if they will live up to the hype, she says.

And don't be blind to the calories and fat in the sweet treats you pick up at such coffee spots as Starbucks, Chin says.

Overall, use common sense and restraint when eating on the run, Chin suggests. "Considering all nutritional aspects, fast-food meals should not be a recommended everyday activity."

8

Slow Foods Offer a Healthy Alternative to Fast Foods

Tufts University Health & Nutrition Letter

The Tufts University Health & Nutrition Letter *provides consumers with honest and scientifically authoritative health and nutrition advice.*

A new movement, called "slow food," has established itself in recent years. Originally started in the 1980s by Carlo Petrini, the movement has emphasized the quality of the dining experience rather than a specific diet. The movement nonetheless believes that by snacking less frequently and by preparing one's own meals, individuals will 1) eat less, 2) eat healthier, less processed, foods, and 3) enjoy eating more. Likewise, individuals should follow similar principles when eating out, choosing restaurants with a relaxed atmosphere and taking time to savor one's food.

On one level, fast food appears to be taking a hit. McDonald's recently announced the closing of 175 restaurants and slashed prices on some popular items to counter flagging sales. Wendy's and other chains are also experiencing weakening profits. But whether or not people turn away from burgers and fries, fast food, in a larger sense, has taken root. Americans now eat fast and drink fast—and often want their meals prepared so fast that they completely bypass cooking.

We think it's a trend in the wrong direction. It's not just that when you let others make your meals for you, they decide how much saturated fat and sodium and how little fiber you eat. It's also that you don't pay attention to your food and end up eating too much. Wolfing something down while driving, working at your desk, or standing at the kitchen counter, you can't "hear" your body telling you when you're full. (It takes 20 minutes, on average, for the brain to notify the stomach that you've had enough.)

Along with a lack of attention, a lack of enjoyment from quick eating gets people consuming more than they should, too. Part of what people seek in a meal is good taste, pleasure, and relaxation. If those elements are missing, eating continues even after hunger is sated in a search for the more intangible satisfaction food is meant to bestow. And that substantially increases the chances for extra pounds to creep on, which raises the incidence of heart disease, diabetes, stroke, and many of the other major conditions that are debilitating—and killing—Americans.

The Slow Food Movement

For those reasons, we feel it's imperative that people consider not just the ingredients in their food but also the circumstances under which they eat. We think there should be a return to slow food, if you will.

It's not a new concept. In fact, there's an organization called Slow Food that now boasts 65,000 members in 45 countries. It was started in the 1980s by an Italian food-and-wine writer named Carlo Petrini to protest the opening of a McDonald's in the heart of Rome.

Slow Food (www.slowfood.com) doesn't actually focus much on nutrition. In fact, much of its focus is rather esoteric for most people's level of interest. For instance, it has offered an entire course on balsamic vinegar. And members of Slow Food's London branch were recently invited to a dinner at which "we will not only taste the fabled Black Trumpet mushroom, but our host. . . will give a talk on the typical fungi of

Slovenia." The reason for such events is that the organization is very much concerned with preserving local traditions in the face of what it refers to as the "standardization" of food across the globe. It also focuses on organic farming, traditional methods of cooking, and saving varieties of fruits and vegetables that are in danger of going extinct. . . .

So where do Slow Food's concerns and those of the average health-conscious American intersect? In Slow Food's strong stand for the "protection of the right to taste"; in its belief that meals are meant to be enjoyed rather than simply swallowed; in its conviction that people would get more out of preparing their own food than from always having strangers prepare it for them. If more people used those principles as guides, their meals would automatically become more healthful.

Slow Food Tenets

To that end, here are seven slow-food guidelines of our own, all in keeping with the tenets of the Slow Food movement. We believe they make good resolutions for the New Year—and for always.

Americans average 22 hours of television watching a week, so there's definitely some time to cook.

---

1. Don't eat unless you're sitting at a table. You're not so likely to feel you've eaten a satisfying amount of food when, for instance, you have ice cream out of the container while standing in the kitchen. A little bit keeps turning into a little bit more. Better to scoop some ice cream into a dish, put the container back in the freezer, walk over to the table, sit down, and eat (at a relaxed pace) the portion that seemed appropriate when you dished it out.

2. Prepare more of your own meals. If you never make your own dinner, try doing it once a week. If you do it twice a

week, shoot for three times. You eat much more healthfully when you cook than when you eat out, take out, or order in. When put to the task of preparing dinner, most people intuitively include a vegetable or two (frozen is fine) to go along with a protein (like fish, chicken, beef, or beans) and a starch (like rice, potatoes, barley, or bulgur)—which is perfect.

Don't believe you don't have time to prepare your own meals. That's a bill of goods people are sold by marketers to get them to buy pre-prepared stuff. Americans average 22 hours of television watching a week, so there's definitely some time to cook.

3. Don't eat when you're not hungry. This is a tough one in a culture where boredom, anxiety, fatigue, TV ads, and food on every corner beget eating. But it's worth paying attention to. When people eat in the absence of hunger, they often eat guiltily, which means quickly—too quickly to stop before the calories really pile up.

Note: Do not tell yourself you'll just eat less later. You won't. A series of elegantly conducted studies in France (where else?) has shown that snacking unaccompanied by hunger doesn't reduce the number of calories eaten at the next meal a few hours later.

4. Savor what you're eating. When you eat quickly and inattentively, you lose out on a lot of food's flavor. Consider that much of what we think of as taste is really smell. The taste buds can only detect a few things: salty, bitter, sour, and sweet. But as a person chews, a food's volatiles—odorous, gas-like substances—are released and "pumped" to the nose. There are literally thousands of odors that the human nose can distinguish. It's what allows you to tell the difference between, say, cinnamon and nutmeg or chicken and turkey. The less you chew, however, the less you're going to be able to appreciate those differences.

Of course, when you eat too fast, your taste buds get short shrift, too. Fast food companies are well aware of that, says

Rosemary Stanton, PhD, a leading nutritionist in Australia. They purposely make their foods soft and moist so their menu items hardly need any chewing and can be eaten fast as well as purchased fast (think burgers with greasy dressing that almost dissolve between the tongue and the roof of the mouth, she says). But the chains compensate for the fact that their offerings hardly need any time in the mouth by using a lot of salt, sugar, and fat (the latter for mouthfeel). Thus, even brief contact with the taste buds and minimal release of volatile odors ensure a flavor hit. Foods that move through the mouth more slowly, Dr. Stanton notes, don't need so much of those ingredients to satisfy.

5. Don't eat what you don't like. It would seem obvious, but it's not. Who hasn't had the fruit-flavored chocolates because they're the only ones left in the box when they really prefer the ones with nuts? What a waste of calories, not to mention satisfaction.

6. Follow the same principles in restaurants that you would at home. You should expect the same relaxed atmosphere in a restaurant as in your own kitchen or dining room. If you feel rushed by the waitstaff; if you have to roar above the din to have a conversation; if you don't feel comfortable asking for special requests, like for some of your entree to be packed in a doggie bag before it ever reaches your table, you're not in the right place.

7. Participate in some moderately vigorous physical activity each day. What does this have to do with slow food? Everything. Exercise helps with appetite control. Also, if you move your body appropriately, you'll want to fuel it appropriately instead of eating willy-nilly whatever's available. You'll take the time to plan, prepare, and partake of good-tasting, nutritious meals. In other words, one good behavior builds on another.

9

Dieting Causes Children to Gain Weight

Jennifer Warner

Jennifer Warner is a writer and wine educator based in Hawke's Bay wine country, New Zealand.

While many children diet today, a recent study found that they might actually gain more weight than children who do not diet. Dieting, the study found, often promotes unhealthy eating habits that remain into adulthood. Dieting also increases the likelihood of binge eating. Instead of dieting, children need to develop healthy eating habits, including eating a variety of healthy foods, and increasing physical activity, including spending less time in front of the television and computer.

Oct. 6, 2003–Children and teens who constantly go on and off diets to lose weight may actually end up gaining extra pounds in the long run.

A new study shows that girls who were frequent dieters gained about two extra pounds per year, and boys who were dieters gained more than two extra pounds per year compared with nondieters.

Researchers say the findings show that putting overweight children on restrictive diets not only doesn't help them lose weight, but it also promotes unhealthy eating habits that can last a lifetime.

For example, the study showed that girls who were frequent dieters were 12 times more likely than nondieters to en-

Jennifer Warner, "Dieting May Promote Weight Gain in Kids," *WebMD Medical News*, October 6, 2003. © 2005–2006 WebMD, Inc. All rights reserved. Reproduced by permission.

gage in binge eating, and boys who dieted were seven times more likely to become binge eaters.

Children and Dieting Don't Mix

For the study, researchers followed a group of 8,200 girls and 6,770 boys for three years starting in 1996. They were 9 to 14 years of age. Participants filled out annual questionnaires about dieting, weight change, exercise, and eating habits.

Researchers found that nearly 30% of the girls and 16% of the boys were dieters at the start of the study. During the three-year follow-up, the study showed that dieters consistently gained more weight than nondieters, with dieters gaining an average of nearly two more pounds per year more than nondieters.

Dieters were also much more likely to engage in binge eating, defined as eating large amounts of food in a short period of time and feeling out of control in the situation—such as eating an entire box of cookies and feeling that you couldn't stop even if you wanted to.

"What we think is happening is that the more frequently they dieted, the more frequently they would binge eat or overeat in between these dieting episodes, and that would lead to their weight gain," says researcher Alison Field, ScD, assistant professor at Harvard Medical School.

Field says this study is among the first to look at the long-term effect of dieting in children and teens, and the findings show that it's wrought with many of the same problems that affect adults who try to lose weight with the latest fad diet.

"Diets are very hard to stick with because most people pick a diet that's going to make them really lose weight and notice changes very rapidly," Field tells WebMD. "Unfortunately, what we really should be recommending is something where you're not going to see the results as quickly, but it's easier to adhere to."

That means making smaller, more modest changes, like changing from a 20-ounce bottle of Coke to a 12-ounce can, or changing from eating super-sized portions to normal-sized portions.

Dieting Alone Isn't Enough

Pediatrician Michael Wasserman, MD, says the findings aren't surprising, because losing weight takes more than just dieting in both children and adults.

"The answer is not that dieting is bad, but that changing your lifestyle is a better way," says Wasserman, who works at a child weight-loss program at the Ochsner Clinic Foundation in New Orleans.

"It has to be a multifactorial change in how you live. You just can't change one piece of it, you need to change the whole day-to-day lifestyle that the youngster goes through," Wasserman tells WebMD.

Research also shows that children who are overweight or obese have a 90% chance of being overweight as an adult.

But Wasserman also points out that 90% of the study participants were white and they all were children of nurses who participated in the Nurses Health Study II, so the results might not apply to the entire population.

Even so, the study highlights the need for parents to strike a healthy balance between encouraging healthy eating habits and not making food an emotional issue, which could lead to potentially dangerous binge eating or eating disorders.

Smart Ways to Help Kids Lose Weight

How to help children and teens lose weight is a problem more and more parents are facing today as the prevalence of overweight children has risen by 100% in the last 20 years. Currently about 15% of children and adolescents are overweight or obese.

Research also shows that children who are overweight or obese have a 90% chance of being overweight as an adult, and that's why experts say it's important to help children develop healthy habits as early as possible. Having obese parents also increases the risks that the child will be obese.

Registered dietitian Rachel Brandeis offers the following tips to help children (and their parents) attain and maintain a healthy weight:

- *Get moving.* Increasing physical activity to burn more calories is the best way to encourage weight loss in children. Turn off the TV or computer and get them involved in any type of sporting activity.

- *Offer a variety of healthy foods.* Limit sugary snacks, sweets, and other sources of empty calories, such as potato chips.

- *Don't label foods.* Labeling a food as "bad" is likely to make that food more appealing to children and might lead to overeating or binging when it becomes available at home or elsewhere.

- *Avoid "family style" meals.* Plating foods in the kitchen gives parents more control over portion size and helps children learn what a kid-sized portion should look like.

Brandeis says it's also important for parents to set a healthy example for their kids with their own eating habits.

"Children model parent's behaviors. So if parents are constantly talking about being on a diet, and saying, 'I can't eat this, I can't eat that,' children pick up on those patterns as well," Brandeis tells WebMD.

"Food should just be healthy," says Brandeis, who is a spokeswoman for the National Dietetic Association. "There's room for treats, there's room for empty calories, but if your child is struggling with a weight issue . . . don't make food such a big issue."

10

Children Need an Age-Appropriate Diet

Sharon Dalton

Sharon Dalton is an associate professor in the Department of Nutrition, Food Studies, and Public Health at New York University, and the author of Overweight and Weight Management: The Health Professional's Guide to Understanding and Practice.

Children rarely benefit from restrictive diets. Instead, parents should concentrate on weight management, a method that allows an overweight child to "grow into" his or her weight. A seven-year-old child should simply eat like a seven-year-old child, drawing the recommended servings and serving sizes from the Food Guide Pyramid. Many children, however, eat excessive portions, and many of the foods they eat are high in fat and sugar content. Families need to reduce both the portions and number of servings that make up a child's diet, and slowly replace foods high in fat and sugar content with healthier ones. Over time, new habits and goals can help maintain a healthier diet.

In whatever course I teach, talk I give, or workshop I lead, the recurrent questions about weight management programs are, what *really* works, and *how long* does it take? To both, the answer is that it depends. It depends on how we measure what works or what is effective; it depends on children's genetic background, age, and growth rate, as well as their home and social environment. There is no simple or easy answer, though many parents desperately wish there were.

I can say with more certainty what does *not* work for kids: restrictive diets. By restrictive diets, I mean eating plans that strictly curb the amount and type of food permitted. There is little, if any, evidence that they work. Most short-term weight loss cancels itself out, and restriction generally leads to nagging parents, anxious kids, and bad long-term results.

Drawing on a huge amount of research and experience in adult obesity, most experts agree that success in combating obesity depends on long-term *weight management*, not a "diet." Weight management is not just weight loss. Management also means rethinking individual behavior and choices to sustain a healthy weight with balanced eating and physical activity, day in and day out. This is much more difficult than "going on a diet" for a few weeks.

Traditionally the term *diet* referred to what we eat every day, which over time becomes an eating pattern. Using available, affordable, and acceptable foods, culture shapes our diet. In the past quarter century, however, the term took on a specific and sometimes pejorative sense of a short-term restrictive eating plan whose goal is weight loss. When most people consider obesity treatment, they mistakenly plan short-term penance, not lifelong weight management.

If an overweight child maintains her weight as she grows, her weight and height will come back into line.

What follow are several questions and my answers related to dieting and weight management. These are typical of questions I field from parents, educators, and health providers as they seek to help seriously overweight youth reach and keep a healthier weight.

Healthy Dieting for Children

Should a five-year-old overweight child be on a diet?

No, a five-year-old overweight child should eat like a five-year-old healthy-weight child, not like an eighteen-year-old basketball player.

I do not endorse weight reduction for children—except for extremely overweight seven to eleven-year-olds and teens with health complications—but I do support weight maintenance, which stalls excess weight gain and allows overweight children to "grow into" their weight. Children don't need diets; they need to eat for their age and be moderately active. Guidelines endorsed by the American Academy of Pediatrics say that, for overweight children ages two to seven, the goal is weight maintenance, not weight loss. If an overweight child maintains her weight as she grows, her weight and height will come back into line.

If a nine-year-old child is so overweight that his blood pressure is high and he has sleep apnea (breathing difficulty), should he be on a diet to lose weight?

First, the family's healthy eating and activity should stop the weight gain. Then, changes in eating and activity should aim toward a weight loss of about one pound per month.

What are the changes in eating required to stop the weight gain or to lose a pound or two a month?

This question usually means, "I want a diet that works." I hear it from parents, and I hear it from lots of health professionals. "You're a dietitian; give her a diet." Again, I give my standard answer, "A seven-year-old should eat like a seven-year-old. Choose foods from all parts of the Food Guide Pyramid in the *amounts* recommended for her age and activity."

That sounds too easy. Why are kids still getting fatter?

After I find out what a child usually eats and we compare samples of the recommended amounts with his usual daily diet, I try to bring the family's idea of normal amounts in line with reality. After some probing into what and how much he ate yesterday, or any day in general, I may find that this seven-year-old overweight child has been eating like a seventeen-year old. His reported daily menu, like Dwayne's, may look something like this:

Reasonable and Unreasonable Daily Menus

Before school: a large glass of orange juice (12 oz); Froot Loops (3/4 cup) with whole milk (1 cup); and one jelly doughnut

Snack at school (brought from home): Snapple drink (12 oz); potato chips (6 oz bag); mozzarella cheese stick

Lunch served at school: pepperoni pizza (2 slices) and whole milk (8 oz)

After-school snack: large serving of fries with three packs of ketchup; soda (12 oz)

Supper: two pieces deep-fried chicken; rice and beans (about 1 cup); three bites (1 tablespoon) carrots; two glasses of soda (20 oz)

TV time: large bowl of chocolate ice cream (1 cup)

Snack before bed: sweetened applesauce (3/4 cup) and one chocolate graham cracker

Throughout the day: M&M candy (4 oz bag)

Total calories for day (approximately): 3,200

In one day Dwayne takes in foods from all parts of the Food Guide Pyramid in at least the minimum number of recommended servings (counting the fries, ketchup, and pizza tomato sauce as vegetables, the double-size orange juice and applesauce as three fruit servings). But he also takes in about 3,200 calories. The estimated daily calorie requirement is about 1,800 calories for a moderately active seven-year-old boy with a healthy weight-for-height. The range is 1,400 to 2,400 calories depending on activity and appropriate growth rate. Dwayne does not need "a diet." Dwayne needs to eat like a seven-year-old and to spend at least an hour a day in moderate to vigorous physical activity—like a seven-year-old!

Dwayne's food choices are not necessarily "bad" (though they could use improvement in the high-fat and sugar department); the main problem is they are "big." Eating the recommended number of servings in the recommended serving sizes would give Dwayne a great start for improving his daily diet and for slimming down as he grows up. Tilting his food choices toward less-calorie-packed foods would make his diet healthier and give him an excellent chance to have fewer chronic diseases as he grows up.

With a few modifications, Dwayne's daily diet can be adjusted to provide approximately 1,800 calories from foods that he finds acceptable—and that meet the guidelines for a child his age. From a nutrition education perspective, these changes appear relatively easy and painless; but Dwayne and his family may think they are very restrictive, like a "diet." The goal, then, is to include the same foods he usually eats but in smaller amounts and gradually change the type, such as moving from whole to low-fat milk, from jelly doughnuts to toast and jelly. To help him learn choices, foods are grouped as "anytime" (carrots, rice, and beans), "sometimes" (soda, ice cream) and "seldom" (fries, doughnuts, M&Ms). Dwayne and his family will decide (with guidance) how to interpret "sometimes" and "seldom." A sample day might look like this:

Before school: small glass of orange juice (8 oz); Wheaties topped with Froot Loops or lightly sweetened Cheerios (1 oz), with 1 percent low-fat milk; toast and jelly

Snack: apple, banana, or kiwi, or 100 percent fruit juice (6 oz); water; mozzarella stick or peanut butter spread on 2 low-fat Triscuits

Lunch: vegetable (broccoli) pizza (2 slices); low-fat milk (1 cup); unsweetened applesauce (4 oz)

After-school snack: Lite canned fruit (1/2 cup) or 100 percent fruit juice (8 oz); chocolate graham crackers (2 squares); water

Dinner: oven-baked chicken (3 oz); rice and beans (1 cup); carrots (raw or cooked, 1/2 cup); green and red pepper strips; ice cream (1/2 cup); water

TV time (or family game): popcorn and 12 oz soda

Total calories (approximately): 1,800

Changing Habits and Setting Goals

Will an overweight child like Dwayne actually eat this type of food, everyday?

Yes, unless his family eats most meals from take-out restaurants or vending machines. This sample daily menu does require Dwayne's family to spend a minimal amount of time shopping for groceries and preparing meals and snacks. And with very little effort his family can adopt an eating plan similar to the one outlined above that is acceptable, affordable, and available for Dwayne. It follows nutrition guidelines that represent millions of dollars in educational development and promotional materials (the USDA Food Guide Pyramid for Young Children). But most nutrition education programs stop here. They provide the information. The best programs also tailor the information to an individual's needs and situation, and this plan does that too, for Dwayne, with modified amounts of foods he is used to and a method for choosing among the "seldom" foods that now boost his total calories into the stratosphere for a kid his age.

What is the likelihood that Dwayne will eat according to this plan and slowly grow into his weight?

A very small likelihood—if all we do is "give" his family the diet plan. What is required, experts claim and I agree, is learning to change behavior. To support healthier food choices, Dwayne and his family need to learn skills—shopping to have snacks available rather than going to McDonald's for fries, and cooking with less grease (oven-baked chicken, homemade popcorn with minimal oil). And they need to substitute activities to replace TV time and to encourage them to apply their new skills. For Dwayne, this may involve learning to choose a goal and reward: "If I have only one 'seldom' food each day for at least five days a week, I get to go bowling with my brother" (behavioral contracting); learning to check his degree of hunger, by making a fist, imagining it as his stomach, and counting how many fingers full he feels (stimulus control); or making a chart of how many "seldom" foods he eats a day or number of times a week he turns off the TV for half an hour or more, then reviewing it with a parent (self-monitoring).

The most successful programs for kids are those that enroll both children and families.

For best results, parents should work with their children to make sure the goals they choose are positive, specific, and realistic, like these:

Positive goals: "I will drink more water," not "I will drink less soda"

Specific goal actions: "I will play hopscotch and talk with Anna outside after school for about an hour, three out of five days a week," *not* "I will play more outside games"

Realistic goals: "I will eat raw carrots, which I like (I hate cooked carrots)"

Should a child be in a weight-management treatment program even if the family is not part of it?

The Expert Committee on Obesity Evaluation and Treatment, a group that develops guidelines for the American Academy of Pediatrics, recommends that when a family believes obesity is inevitable or resists efforts to modify activity or meals, the treatment of an overweight child should be deferred until the family is ready to change; or the family should be referred to a therapist who can address the family's readiness. "Lack of readiness will probably lead to failure, which will frustrate the family and perhaps prevent future weight-control efforts." The committee further recommends that the whole family be required to participate "in creating new family behaviors consistent with the child's new eating and activity goals." Otherwise, regular caregivers who do not participate in these changes may undermine the treatment program.

The most successful programs for kids are those that enroll both children and families. In fact, one program that targeted the parents exclusively—and not the child—found that improved parenting skills brought about the child's weight loss. . . .

Are there successful plans and programs—commercial or based in health clinics—that are safe for kids and that work over the long term?

It is difficult to say. An untold number of obesity treatment plans for children and adults crowd the marketplace, and some are better than others. . . .

A specific program's effectiveness is hard to gauge. To most kids and parents, effectiveness usually means that the program enabled participants to lose weight and keep it off. To program providers, effectiveness usually means that some participants stopped gaining weight and improved one or two eating and activity behaviors. I think effectiveness should involve maintaining weight as a child grows (not weight loss) and meeting one or two realistic behavior goals each week.

The Ups and Downs of Self-Monitoring

Should parents who seek to slow their overweight child's weight gain keep daily logs that detail how much the child eats and exercises?

Many weight-management programs recommend record keeping or "self-monitoring," to keep track of and then analyze the eating and exercise behavior patterns. For overweight kids, this can be a drag and a nag point for their parents. It is better to agree on a goal and reward, such as eat only one "seldom" food most days and spend time with positive activities (like Dwayne's "go bowling with my brother") rather than laborious writing. That said, record keeping relates to greater success for adults in weight management. There is no evidence for kids.

Self-monitoring involves recording what you eat; what's happening (or not happening) before and during eating; and what happens after eating. The idea is to figure out the *antecedents, behavior,* and *consequences* of your eating patterns. These are the "ABCs" of your food and eating environment. The first tells what the triggers are to what you eat ("it's there"; "Gramma insisted I eat it"). The second tells how much and what kind of food ("two slices of pizza; two 12 oz colas"). The third tells how you feel and what happens after you eat it ("I felt stuffed and mad at myself"). Learning what happens helps children handle the antecedents the next time in order to change unwanted behavior and consequences. A positive "ABC" could be "try to have watermelon in fridge," "ate a big slice," "felt full and healthy." The theory is that reinforcing this positive pattern by repeating it will lead to new, healthier behavior (it can also apply to goals for physical activity). That's the upside of self-monitoring. The downside is that such a close and continual analysis of self-behavior could lead to more obsessive and overcontrolling behavior. Parents can play to the positive parts (revelations and rewards) while discouraging the negative (fixation with every bite of food).

11

Dieting Leads to Eating Disorders

Diane Guernsey

Diane Guernsey is a columnist for Town & Country.

Many teenagers diet in hopes of improving self-esteem and social standing, only to develop unhealthy eating habits. As a result, a number of teens also develop eating disorders including bulimia, a condition often marked by binge eating followed by purging. Continued over time, bulimia can potentially lead to a number of health problems, including damaging one's heart. Therapy is often helpful in changing these behaviors and helping individuals build a healthier relationship with food.

It all began with the Grapefruit Diet. I was thirteen, growing up in Southern California. Little did I know that my first attempt at weight loss would set me on the path to bulimia—a path shadowed in shame and secrecy. Only now, more than twenty-five years later, can I look back and map the road I took through those shadows and back into health.

About the diet: I didn't understand what I was getting into. I thought I was entering a brave new world where, ten pounds thinner, I would become socially fluent and self-confident. This was a stretch: although I had good friends and hobbies I was passionate about, I was also shy, bookish and uncomfortable in my own skin—not exactly Popular Girl material. But I blamed all my social unease on being slightly overweight—I was five foot eight and 140 pounds. If only that were different. . . .

Unfortunately, strict dieting led not to Nirvana but to an endless cycle: lose five pounds, gain five pounds; repeat. My fierce self-deprivation while following what my mother called "those crazy diets" also spurred me to binge eat rebelliously, so for two years my weight stayed put.

Then a friend mentioned how some girls made themselves vomit to keep from gaining weight. I recoiled. Some time after that, though, I panicked and resorted to this bizarre weight-control method. My disgust with myself was outweighed only by the relief of having (as I thought) fended off fatness.

I learned that it had a medical name—bulimia—and that I was risking heart damage or worse. But I couldn't stop.

Gradually, purging became an integral part of my life—something I wasn't sure I could stop, and definitely something I couldn't tell anyone about. Looking in the mirror, I couldn't match that curvaceous but normal-looking fifteen-year-old girl with someone who would do such a monstrous thing. I shoved the knowledge deep down and tried to forget it.

Losing Control

Then, during my last year of high school, my life blew apart. My family moved across the country, whisking me away from my much-loved friends and into a small, snobbish school that had no place for me. Completely unprepared for the crushing sense of grief and loss, I began, blindly, furiously, to binge eat—a desperate, unconscious attempt to mute the crazy-making pain. In three months I gained forty pounds. Predictably, too, I began purging daily, often more than once, trying to undo the damage.

It was my worst nightmare come true. As agonizing as it was to feel totally out of control, it was even worse to feel consumed by self-loathing. No one else could possibly have despised me as much as I despised myself in those days.

I told no one about my purging. (My parents were horrified enough by my weight gain; I couldn't imagine what they'd say about this.) I learned that it had a medical name—bulimia—and that I was risking heart damage or worse. But I couldn't stop.

In my junior year at college, I used the money I'd earned working in the library to see a psychotherapist, who helped me grapple with some of my deepest fears—of leaving home, of social situations, of failing to find a place in the world—but he couldn't directly help me with my purging, because I felt too ashamed to tell him about it. Even so, the behavior subsided a bit.

Emboldened by my success, I sought more help. During graduate school, I entered group therapy—and discovered that the other women there also struggled with food and eating. (Still, I didn't confide my own problem.) I attended workshops on women and food. I read Susie Orbach's *Fat Is a Feminist Issue* and Geneen Roth's *Feeding the Hungry Heart*, both of which explore how women use food, eating and weight to express (or suppress) painful feelings about their lives, relationships and gender roles. In a support group centered on this idea, I took my first tottery steps toward "no-fault," mindful eating: eating only when I was hungry, eating exactly what I wanted (be it dessert or steak), focusing on the food, stopping when I was full.

My bingeing and purging tapered off tremendously, and by grace or good luck, I had been spared bulimia's health ravages. But I still had more to learn. At twenty-eight, I embarked on intensive psychoanalysis, and, finally, I shared my secret.

The relief was indescribable. My therapist calmly went about trying to understand the feelings, thoughts and events that had led to my behavior. Within months I stopped purging altogether.

Nowadays I've reached a basic equilibrium vis-a-vis food (well, most of the time—nobody's perfect). I truly love food, especially when I eat with attention. I also forget about food when I'm caught up in work; and, like most people, I sometimes overeat just because, or at holiday meals. The pain is gone, leaving room for freedom—even delight.

One moment when I knew I was truly getting well took place, in fact, at a *Town & Country* holiday party. Faced with a tray of fancy chocolate truffles, I neither flinched nor felt compelled to eat them all. I took one carefully in my fingers, nibbled it slowly, savoring every morsel down to the last, and was content.

12

A Vegetarian Diet Does Not Lead to Eating Disorders

Carol LaLiberte

Carol LaLiberte is a college instructor and writer.

Because a number of teens with eating disorders limit certain types of food, including meat, people have equated bulimia and anorexia nervosa with vegetarianism. But bulimia and anorexia have many causes, including depression, and there appears to be no connection between eating disorders and vegetarianism. The American Dietetic Association states that a well-planned vegetarian diet is healthy and may even prevent certain diseases. The confusion concerning eating disorders and vegetarianism nonetheless persists because a number of teens quit eating meat in an attempt to lose weight. These teens, sometimes referred to as "pseudo-vegetarians" by physicians, may also limit other foods, and should not be confused with teens who have chosen a vegetarian lifestyle.

If you are a parent of a teen, particularly a vegetarian teen, then perhaps reading the opening line that appeared in a recent newspaper article left you stunned, confused, or concerned. It read, "Teenage vegetarians may be at greater risk of eating disorders and suicide than their meat eating peers, according to researchers." You might be wondering if it is, in fact, true.

Those headlines caught my eye as well. I am a college professor who has watched too many young women starving themselves in the course of the semester during which they had me for their teacher. One woman in particular was one of the most attractive females I have ever met. She was bright and bubbly on the outside while inside she was dying a little every day. She was greatly disturbed and several times was hospitalized during the semester, each time returning to class afterwards only to hand in exemplary papers and earn perfect scores on exams. By the end of the semester she could barely walk into class unaided, a mere sheath of skin covering her bones. Her excessive dieting had nothing at all to do with vegetarianism. I didn't need research to tell me that. Her diet was not well balanced or eaten for health and well-being nor for the protection of animals. She followed the dietary regime that she did because she was striving for perfection in all aspects of her life and had a warped sense of her physical appearance. She did eliminate her intake of all animal products as well as nearly all other food groups. She was not a vegetarian but a person who desperately needed help.

Eating Disorders

The two most common eating disorders are anorexia nervosa, or self-starvation, and bulimia, or bingeing combined with purging. Eating disorders are more common in teen girls than boys, and even as early as fourth grade, girls are more likely than boys to be worried about their weight. One in 200 American adolescents have anorexia nervosa and three out of one hundred have bulimia (American Psychological Association 1994). About half of anorexics also have bulimia. Girls who have anorexia reduce their food intake so extremely that they lose 15 percent of their body weight. They fear gaining weight so much so that they starve themselves to death. Even when they are dying from starvation and extreme deprivation and thinness, their perception is still that they are too fat. About 10 percent of anorexics die from either starvation or the physical problems resulting from it.

Bulimics usually maintain a normal weight because in between their bingeing and purging they maintain normal eating habits. Similar to anorexics, bulimics do fear weight gain but unlike anorexics, they view their bingeing and purging as abnormal behavior.

With guidance in meal planning, vegetarian diets are appropriate and healthful choices for adolescents.

Eating disorders are more common in cultures that emphasize thinness, especially Western countries. Also, girls living in middle to upper socioeconomic classes are more likely to have eating disorders as a result of the focus on striving for a slim figure. Eating disorders are most common in teens and early twenties when girls are paying most attention to media messages of what is a perfect figure and identifying with expectations about what it means to be a beautiful female in their culture. Females who have eating disorders often have other disorders as well, particularly depression. Warm but highly controlling parents can also play a role in a young woman's striving to be physically perfect.

A Vegetarian Diet and Eating Disorders

The ADA states, "It is the position of The American Dietetic Association that appropriately planned vegetarian diets are healthful, are nutritionally adequate, and provide health benefits in the prevention and treatment of certain diseases." They go on to state that "well-planned vegan and lacto-ovo-vegetarian diets are appropriate for all stages of the life cycle. Vegetarian diets are somewhat more common among adolescents with eating disorders than in the general adolescent population; therefore, dietetics professionals should be aware of young clients who greatly limit food choices and who exhibit symptoms of eating disorders. However, *recent data suggest that adopting a vegetarian diet does not lead to eating dis-*

orders. With guidance in meal planning, vegetarian diets are appropriate and healthful choices for adolescents."

Currently there is no connection between vegetarian diets and eating disorders such as bulimia and anorexia nervosa. Recent research from Australia and the United States shows that after the onset of anorexia teens claim to have given up eating meat, however, they also claim to have given up many other foods as well, thereby leaving them in an unhealthy state. This study found that some young women are using vegetarianism as an excuse to avoid eating certain foods. Doctors are now making the distinction between these young women and those who are vegetarians in order to maintain good health and referring to the former as pseudo-vegetarians.

As it turns out, looking beyond the claim that a teen is a vegetarian is a very important thing for parents and others to do. Nutrition experts at UT Southwestern Medical Center at Dallas say that parents whose teens want to eat a vegetarian diet should not be overly concerned. Rather this would be a good time to explore together what constitutes a healthy diet and perhaps consult with a dietician or nutritionist who is versed in preparing well balanced, nutritious, vegetarian diets. Pseudo-vegetarians or teens who are adopting a non-meat-eating regime solely to restrict intake and lose or control weight deserve and require psychological intervention.

13

Dieting Prolongs the Adult Lifespan

Julia Sommerfeld

Julia Sommerfeld is a staff writer for the Seattle Times.

A number of dieters have reduced their calorie intake by 30% or more in the belief that fewer calories will increase the body's resistance to disease and prolong aging. While no long-term studies have been conducted on humans, calorie reduction has been shown to increase the life span of animals. Reducing calories, however, also leaves individuals with less energy, and may be less healthy for older adults who are losing muscle mass. While current research may eventually prove the benefits of calorie reduction, individual practitioners, convinced of the results, have been reducing calories for a number of years. The earlier they start, the reasoning goes, the more years will be added to their lives.

Before taking up his fork, Micky Snir eyes his dinner plate solemnly, as if his life depends on it. In fact, that's what he's counting on.

It's his 38th birthday and his indulgence at Claim Jumper, a Redmond restaurant known for towering stacks of barbecue ribs, is a salmon fillet with the breading scraped off. He eats only part of the fish but dives into the side of steamed vegetables, more in keeping with the Spartan diet he's followed for two years.

The Microsoft software engineer figures that by subsisting on about 2,000 calories a day—nearly 30 percent less than recommended for a man as active as he is—he will tack an extra 15 years onto his life. "I think of it as a living savings account. Instead of eating everything I want now, I save calories so when I'm old I get to live a few more years," he says.

It's a brand of dietary providence foreign to the typical tubby American. But Snir is no crackpot. His regimen has 70 years of science behind it.

Study after study in worms, flies, spiders, guppies, yeast, mice and rats shows slashing calorie intake by about 30 percent lengthens life span by about the same percentage. If the strategy works in humans, that would translate into as many as 20 extra years for people. Not only do critters live longer, calorie restriction, or CR as it's known among rodent-starving scientists, also appears to be a panacea for age-related ills. It staves off diabetes, high blood pressure, heart disease, cancer and Alzheimer's.

But the diet may cause problems of its own, such as weakened bones. Researchers are now looking at the diet's possible benefits—and risks—for people. Human-trial findings can't come soon enough for Snir, who learned about the diet while surfing life-extension Web sites. "We'd have to wait a lifetime to get a definitive answer," he says. "So at some point I just decided to take a leap of faith."

Some longevity researchers say he's making a pretty safe bet; skeptics wisecrack that he'll certainly *feel* like he's living longer.

Scientists don't know exactly how CR [calorie reduction] lengthens lives, but they know it goes beyond the mere health benefits of being thin.

"As if we haven't heard that one before," says Brian Delaney, 40, who runs the Calorie Restriction Society, an online support group for about 1,000 followers of the diet. An American living in Stockholm, Sweden, Delaney has experimented with degrees of CR for a decade, hitting as low as 1,400 calories a day. Now he eats 1,800 calories, which leaves the 5-foot-11-inch man a wispy 135 pounds.

He grumbles that calorie restriction has gotten a bad rap; followers have been lumped with cloners, corpse-freezers and other life-extension "cults." Who's crazy, he asks: baby boomers who spend billions on antioxidants, human-growth hormone injections and $50 wrinkle creams, all with no scientific basis? Or calorie counters who've chosen the "only anti-aging approach backed by mainstream science?"

Diet Like Hibernation

Scientists don't know exactly how CR [calorie reduction] lengthens lives, but they know it goes beyond the mere health benefits of being thin. They compare it to hibernation; physical processes that cause wear and tear on the body are drastically slowed.

One leading theory says it works by curbing cellular pollution. When cellular "factories" convert food to energy, they release byproducts known as free radicals. These biochemical ruffians wreak havoc on cells, genes and tissues and have been blamed for age-related changes ranging from crow's-feet to increased cancer risk. When a body metabolizes fewer calories, it's like a car that uses less fuel—there's less free-radical pollution.

CR also may reduce levels of sugar in the blood, suppress hormones that promote cell growth and rouse genes that promote longevity. Any or all of these factors could play a part in slowing the aging process.

Researcher Mark Mattson's pet theory is the "healthy stress" hypothesis. A neuroscientist at the National Institute on Aging (NIA) in Baltimore, Mattson showed CR protects mouse brain cells from developing Alzheimer's and Parkinson's diseases. He also found that feeding mice every other day extended their lives as much as slashing total calories, even though the mice gorged themselves on feeding days. He took this to mean that hunger, whether temporary or chronic, subjects the body to a healthy form of stress that makes cells hardier. Think of the cardiovascular benefits of wind sprints. Now Mattson is about to test what happens when people eat all their food in a four-hour period and fast the rest of the day.

Mattson, a slight 120 pounds at 5 feet 9 inches tall, skips breakfast and has been counting calories since he began studying CR 20 years ago. He does it not to live longer but because he's convinced it reduces the risk of dreaded diseases.

Research Under Way

Whether calorie restriction extends human life poses a formidable research question. To prove it would require closely following the dietary intake of hundreds or thousands of people for decades. And that assumes subjects would agree to stick to a deprivation diet.

Despite the challenges, the NIA is taking the first step with three pilot studies across the country. The one-year studies will first test whether a 30 percent restricted diet is doable and safe for a few hundred volunteers. Sneaking ice cream won't work; researchers are using a metabolic test to determine exactly how many calories people eat.

While CR may make for a slender, healthy 30-year-old, it may make for an excessively frail elderly person.

Dr. Evan Hadley, an NIA associate director spearheading the research, says they also will examine markers such as blood-sugar levels, blood pressure and free radicals. "The studies won't tell us if calorie restriction makes people live longer but it should give us a clue if the immediate effects in humans parallel what we see in mice," he says.

The best evidence may come instead from our branch-mates on the evolutionary tree. In a laboratory in Poolesville, Md., about 75 monkeys are on a 30 percent restricted diet; another 75 eat as much as they like. The NIA study is in its 16th year and captive monkeys usually live about 25 years, so it's too early to tell if CR will lengthen their lives. But tests already hint at positive trends, including healthier hearts and less cancer among the hungry monkeys.

In the absence of human—or even final monkey—results, scientists are split on whether CR is a reasonable step for humans. Mattson says as long as people commit to the daunting task of getting all their vitamins and minerals despite eating less, he thinks it's a healthy diet.

Dr. Itamar Abrass, head of geriatrics at Harborview Medical Center, isn't so sure. "I think there's a benefit in humans; I'd be surprised if there wasn't," he says. But the devil could be in the details, he says.

Without human studies, no one knows when to start or stop the regimen. Starting before sexual maturation could stunt reproductive development, but waiting too long could reduce the payoff.

And while CR may make for a slender, healthy 30-year-old, it may make for an excessively frail elderly person.

People who are already doing CR are "truly experimenting on themselves," Abrass says. "That's OK, but I certainly wouldn't recommend it."

Diet Downsides Even for a diehard like Snir, the diet has downsides; severe hunger pangs and a lowered libido top the list. His hands are sometimes so cold he has to wear gloves while working on the computer. And he's often low on energy. The biggest sacrifice, he says, was giving up mountain biking because it demanded too much energy. Oh, and then there's cheesecake, which he speaks of wistfully.

But Snir, at 5 feet 10 inches tall and 170 pounds, has managed to avoid the gaunt appearance and weakened bones typical of his CR brethren by eating a lot of protein powder and lifting heavy weights. And he is undeterred. Even if he's hit by a bus tomorrow, forgoing French fries will have been worth it, he says. After battling his weight for most of his adult life, the diet helped him drop 30 pounds. Plus, striving for a longer life, he says, made him realize he'd better make it a life worth living—so he began spending more time with his wife and kids.

His wife, Adi, feeds herself and their four young children a diet full of grains and vegetables, but she doesn't count their calories. She takes Micky's aspiration to live longer as a compliment: "It must mean he likes the life he has with me."

She knows how his regimen must look to outsiders. He weighs nuts and doles them out of pill bottles to make sure he's eating the right amount of protein, and he dines at precisely 10 a.m., 2 p.m., 6 p.m. and 10 p.m. He once barged into the kitchen of an exasperated dinner-party host and grabbed morsels off the stove when a meal wasn't served promptly.

The fact that Snir has stuck with any diet this long, much less one so stringent, sets him apart from most. Knowing how difficult the diet is, many scientists are studying calorie restriction hoping to uncover an age-defying mechanism they can exploit the profitable way—with a pill. No aging cure appears likely within a decade, but already scientists have identified a molecule in red wine that mimics the effects of CR in yeast. They've also spied a gene that seems to change when faced with too-few calories.

But Snir, an ascetic at heart, pooh-poohs the search for a magic pill. "It's like those commercials with the belts that are supposed to shock your belly and give you abs," he says. "Quick fixes never work. People need to be willing to make an effort to make their own lives better."

14

Dieting Is Unhealthy for Older Adults

Harry Jackson Jr.

Harry Jackson Jr. is a reporter for the St. Louis Post-Dispatch.

While dieting has become a national pastime in America, dieting may actually prove a health threat for older Americans. For people under 60, losing weight means losing body fat; for those over 60, losing weight equals losing muscle mass and bone density. Older Americans lose weight for a number of reasons including loss of appetite and dental problems. Excessive weight loss, however, can result in fragile bones and health-related problems. Experts recommend that older adults refrain from weight-loss diets unless they are excessively overweight, and that they continue to exercise, which increases muscle mass and bone density.

One group of people in America might want to ignore all the warnings about the obesity epidemic: people over 60.

After that age, stop dieting, say experts. Losing weight by not eating is dangerous for the elderly, so much so that even nursing homes have stopped serving diets that could promote weight loss, they say. If you want to lose weight, exercise, but don't stop eating.

A few things to remember: Dropping weight for younger people means an effort to reduce body fat. But for older people, losing weight often means dropping muscle mass and bone mass. Also, the chemistry of weight loss can actually make illnesses such as heart disease and other organ diseases worse.

"The body mass index that's healthy for young people is shown to be unhealthy for older people," said Sherry Robinson, assistant professor of nursing at Southern Illinois University School of Medicine in Springfield. "In nursing-home work, we're always watching the weights, because that's the significant problem, weight loss. We're more concerned about weight loss than we are about older people who are overweight."

As baby boomers rewrite the book on aging, they ought not forget that chemistry can't read; the chemistry of people over 60 to 65 changes permanently.

Reasons for Weight Loss

Weight loss among older people can come from a variety of sources, many of them physiological, Robinson said.

Among the causes:

- Often, food loses its appeal. As people age, their senses of smell and taste diminish.

- Older people may have dental problems that make eating more difficult.

- Older people who live alone may be plagued by loneliness, depression and paranoia.

- Medications may reduce appetite or change how people taste food.

- Older people may not be able to afford the foods they found pleasurable before they were on fixed incomes.

- People must deal with the infirmities of age: swallowing problems, glands going haywire or wearing out, and illness.

"It's a huge problem," says Dr. John Morley, director of the department of geriatrics at St. Louis University School of Medicine. "We're so fixated on obesity at the moment. But the problem is that as we get older, if you start to lose weight, you can't carry your weight any more because you're losing muscle weight as well. Then you become what's known as the 'fat frail,' and we've shown in studies that fundamentally, these are the people who have the worst outcomes."

A Change in Chemistry and Malnutrition

The problem comes from a change in chemistry. In old age, the body produces too much of certain chemicals but too little of certain hormones, so the cells in the muscles and bones are unable to maintain themselves. Although physicians can control the problem with medication, older adults should be aware that dropping muscle and bone mass could occur at a dangerous rate when dieting.

Morley covered the issue extensively in the Winter 2004 edition of his magazine, *Successful Aging*. More studies are available in the October/November 2003 issue of *The Journals of Gerontology Series A: Medical Sciences*.

About 10 percent of American seniors—starting at about 60 to 65 years of age—are underweight, and as many as half of the residents of nursing homes may be underweight, says Morley. The National Health and Nutrition Examination Survey says that up to 16 percent of Americans over 65 consume less than 1,000 calories a day, which adds up to malnutrition.

Pointing to a recent study on weight loss in seniors, Morley said that nearly one-third of elder patients who continued to lose weight died, while more than 90 percent survived after reversing their pattern of weight loss. Another study he pointed out showed that hip fractures tended to occur among older people who were dropping pounds, not overweight seniors.

Howard Houghton, assistant professor of clinical psychiatry at the University of Missouri at Columbia School of Medicine, said he has seen malnutrition among the elderly for a long time.

Many of the cases he has seen stem from Alzheimer's disease and anorexia. People with Alzheimer's often forget to eat and lose their ability to use utensils, he said. In addition, "People who got anorexia years ago used to die. Now, they live into old age. The condition is still there, but once they get into old age, they sometimes just stop fighting it."

Maintaining a Healthy Weight

The experts have some tips regarding weight loss in the elderly. For people who are healthy in general:

- Don't go on weight-loss diets unless you are morbidly obese.

- Exercise increases muscle mass and bone density well into old age.

- Watch for weight stability. In older people, dropping five percent of body weight in less than three months signals illness, says Morley. Put them on a scale and see if they're dropping weight, says Houghton. "Gravity doesn't lie." Watch to see if their clothes are fitting like they used to, he said. Look at their faces. Sunken cheeks and eyes are a sign.

- Get annual checkups. "Even if they're healthy, they should be seen once a year by a doctor for a complete checkup," says Houghton.

- Beware of heart-healthy diets. Morley notes that diets that are heart-healthy for younger people may cause heart problems in older adults. A balanced diet is still the best diet. For someone not eating a lot, add high-density food to other foods—cheese, peanut butter and powdered milk, for example.

- Diabetes may be the only exception to the rules. When your blood sugar is out of whack, says Houghton, that's another set of problems. Work with your physician, but still be wary of any radical weight loss by not eating.

15

An Unhealthy Relationship with Food Causes Diet Obsession

Stanley Bing

Stanley Bing is a reporter for Fortune *and author of the novel,* You Look Nice Today.

Although dieting has become a national obsession, people continue to gain weight. The solution: the Fatkins Diet, a diet specially designed to help individuals lose weight and then gain it back. The diet begins with regular meals that include massive quantities of proteins before adding snacks including Krispy Kreme doughnuts. In four short weeks, an individual will be able to complete the weight-loss/weight-gain cycle.

Everywhere you go these days, people are doing two things: getting fatter and dieting. One can only conclude that the more one diets, the fatter one gets. Now we hear of a brand-new regimen that may break that tragic chain. And as a service to you, I'm testing it out.

It's called the Fatkins Diet—it's Atkins plus carbs. It uses the very best insight available to us in modern dietary science. It's easy to live with. And best of all, it works at least as well as any other diet I've ever been on, enabling the practitioner to lose a significant amount of avoirdupois and then, slowly and inexorably, gain it all back until one achieves the optimal weight to begin the diet all over again.

Step One: Self-Awareness. As with any sensible diet, we begin with an assessment of our situation. For men that means taking a look at what your neck size is and what notch of your belt gets the most action. If more of your neck is outside your collar than in, it's time to go Fatkins. Women may regard their shoe size. Do the tops of your insteps spill over onto the sides of your footwear? Fatkins.

Step Two: Hit the Meat Bar. The Atkins Diet, which kept Dr. Atkins lean and mean (presumably even still, now that he's dead), is based on simple nutritional concepts, and it really works. First, as anyone who has not been on a Russian farm eating nothing but potatoes knows, protein is good and carbohydrates are bad. Fruits and vegetables are bad—they're loaded with stinky carbs. Distilled beverages and big, greasy hunks of cholesterol-loaded meats, however, may be taken in any quantity, no matter how outlandish. That leads to some odd conclusions that nevertheless pay off big in weight loss immediately. A small glass of orange juice is your enemy, for instance; a gallon of vodka, gin, or scotch is your friend. This may produce interesting results behavior-wise, particularly in the morning.

An Atkins day might look something like this.

Breakfast: Six eggs, two pounds of bacon, one large glass of Stoli. Net carbs: 0 grams.

Lunch: 48-ounce T-bone, lettuce wedge, bleu-cheese dressing, two bottles of Bombay Sapphire, six Tic-Tacs. Net carbs: two grams (from the Tic-Tacs).

Dinner: Eight pounds of cheese, six lambchops, one bottle Glenfiddich, one cigar. Net carbs: 0 grams.

Late night snack: Two eggs over easy, one six-pound ham. Large martini. Net carbs: 0.5 grams (from the olive).

The next morning you wake up a couple of pounds lighter but with a strange feeling in your head. That's the problem with Atkins. After several weeks on the diet, in which you bore everybody in the world to big, heaving tears with descriptions of what you ate that day, you're slimmer and, at the same time, feel like killing yourself or somebody else, possibly not in that order.

Of course, as Atkins goes on, one may introduce certain vegetables and crustaceae, which were denied you in the early going, while you were fooling your body into eating itself from the inside in search of carbs. Spinach, for example. Shrimp with globs of mayo, also. Eat hearty! Just stay away from fruits and juices, and keep up the heavy consumption of alcohol, except beer, unless you can drink the stuff that looks like beer but tastes like Alka Seltzer.

Step Three: True Fatkins. You're now on the verge of a nervous breakdown. The sight of bacon and eggs makes you want to run screaming naked through the salad bar, grabbing handfuls of verboten vegetables as you go.

Now it's time to introduce the dimension that I believe, with due modesty, I might have invented—selective carbohydrates in massive doses, taken while standing when no one is looking. The idea is to interject certain dietary events between meals: short, intense eating activities done in private—in a virtually parallel universe of ingestive behavior. Assume the existence of all the meals we discuss above, and simply add the following:

Post-breakfast—Two Krispy Kreme doughnuts.

Prelunch—Nuts.

Post-lunch—One low-carb candy bar. These come in a variety of inedible flavors and consistencies. My favorite has the feel of fine, hardening creosote and the subtle taste of mud.

Predinner—Crackers.

Evening snacks—More "candy" bars, nuts, and some kind of flatbread, peanut butter—but no jelly. Jelly is bad!

With, of course, all meals taken as before. You don't want to fall off Atkins.

I'm about four weeks into Fatkins, and by Labor Day my neck should be back to 17 inches, my belt shrinking around my proud, swelling midsection. Then it's off to the store for some suits in time for fall.

There is a great and majestic rhythm to life, is there not?

16

French Diets Are Healthier than American Diets

Will Clower

Will Clower is the author of The Fat Fallacy: The French Diet Secrets to Permanent Weight Loss *and* The French Don't Diet Plan: 10 Simple Steps to Stay Thin for Life.

Americans have continued to follow the same logic in relation to diets and weight loss, and have continued, despite their efforts, to face the same obstacles. Only by subverting traditional logic and breaking time-held rules will Americans be able to free themselves from ineffective dieting strategies. The typical French diet includes many foods that Americans consider unhealthy, but the obesity rate in France is only 8 percent. Cultural tradition supports a healthy lifestyle in France, one that promotes a more relaxed approach to dining and avoids in-between meal snacks. The answer to the dilemma of American weight loss, then, is a return to basics.

Rabbit was lost. He had that terrible, sinking feeling. No doubt about it, every time he marched Piglet and Pooh into the mists of the Hundred-Acre Wood, they ended up facing the same sand pit. He had tried to be clever and strand Tigger in the woods to curtail his socially inappropriate bouncing. But it was Rabbit and his less zealous conspirators who had become confused and lost.

Pooh, however, was led to his larder by a force of gravitation centered about his belly and, in a fit of crystal clear

Poohian logic, made the winning suggestion. "Since we walk away from the sand pit looking for home . . . and we always end up back at this sand pit . . . perhaps when we get out of sight of this sand pit . . . well, we should try to find it again. Maybe then we should reach home." Rabbit, frustrated by his inability to complete his dubious plan to discipline Tigger, was in no mood for Pooh's fluff-brained ideas. In the end, though, Rabbit remained lost, bouncily rescued by Tigger. Pooh found home.

American Diet Logic

Americans, however hard they work at it, keep searching for a way out of their weight problems, and keep ending up back at the same sand pit. But what if one were to take Pooh at his word? What if one were to do what the American system says would make you good and fat, walk away from what we "know" about weight problems, and then try to find it again?

What would it take to design a diet that would be sure to get you back to the sand pit and make you totally fat? First, you would break the cardinal strictures of both schools of di-etetic thought: don't avoid fats *or* carbohydrates. For example, you might give yourself full-fat cheeses, whole milk, half-and-half in your coffee, and normal butter (not something with "food product" in the title). Have some empty alcohol calories while you are at it by drinking a touch of wine with your meal. Besides, it goes well with the fresh breads you'll eat for lunch and dinner. Don't be obsessed with exercise; just get out of the house once in a while. Eat late at night and don't have a gigantic breakfast. Maybe take an afternoon nap.

There. The perfect prescription. You'll be big as a house in no time. This, though, as you've probably guessed, is exactly the French diet. The country with an 8% obesity rate! I set up this scenario facetiously, but laughed out loud when I later read the chapter entitled, "The Worst Diet in the World," in a very popular recent diet book. As erudite and confident as

Rabbit, the author states that poor health and obesity result from a diet full of "breads and pastries . . . cheese, butter, cream, and other whole-milk products . . . [that] get more butterfat into people's systems for good atherogenic measure."

How can the French violate our established dietary rules by eating fats and carbohydrates, without becoming totally fat and unhealthy?

These predictions of gloom and doom, though, fall flat in front of one simple observation: ordinary French people. They're not fat, heart diseased, and their average life span is greater than ours. One clever theory, felled by the plain upright facts.

French Diet Intuition

What the French do right in regard to food and weight doesn't have as much to do with the percent of this or that in their daily intake content of the food web pyramid scheme blabiddy blah, as it does with common sense cultural habits. And you don't have to be afraid of your food or neurotic about calories either. Of course, no one's suggesting you spend all afternoon in a muumuu shoving down cream-filled, fudge-covered Ding Dongs. The prescription of *what* you eat must be balanced with the equally important issue of *when* and *how* you eat. *Diet* isn't so simplistic that you can just sum up the molecular composition of your food. It involves the larger sense of the word—snacking habits, eating routines, and social rules around the table. These suggestions introduce function as well as form, the style of eating as well as the nature of the food.

With this in mind, now we can address the main question. How can the French violate our established dietary rules by eating fats and carbohydrates, without becoming totally fat and unhealthy? The answer, though, is disarmingly simple and do-able. It doesn't emerge from some elegant high-tech Eureka! revelation or miracle cure that melts your fat away with crystals or magnets. It stems from basic rules we've probably all heard growing up. Here are some starters.

Take smaller bites. Don't snack between meals. Finish what you have in your mouth before putting something else in there. Get outside and walk around. Take your time at the table and talk to the people you are eating with. Have some meats, some vegetables, some breads, some desserts—a little of many things is better than a lot of just one. These are simple rules. Very Pooh.

A New Diet Solution

American nutritionists face weight issues like Rabbit: complex and confusing. The French face them more like Pooh: natural and intuitive. However, despite a thousand Rabbit-like theories, our approach has unfortunately failed to give us any less obesity. In fact, it hasn't even slowed the yearly increases: we can't seem to maintain our current levels of obesity! We try a new diet, circle around again, and find ourselves back at the same sand pit looking for the next hare-brained plan to get us out again.

I believe the solution is simpler than we think. Have you ever rummaged through the fridge for something you knew was there, but just couldn't find? You look behind and under things, rifling through the wilting leftovers in the back, only to find it front row center the whole time—right in front of your nose! The same is true for our diet. After looking so hard for so long, it's time to step back and reconsider what we think we know. First things first.

The Fat Fallacy calls for a clear-headed return to basics. Remember what we have traded in for the impressive complexities of American dietary theories. In two simple components, the French diet takes off weight without even trying. First, don't fear a normal level of fat in your diet. . . . Second, adopt eating habits that foster lower weight and a greater appreciation of the food you do eat. In combination, this dietary approach leaves Rabbit's hyper-complexity spinning somewhere out on its own, and takes common sense by the hand on the way to a healthy form for ourselves in the mists.

17

Dieting Is Linked to Increased Wealth

Ascribe Health News Service

Ascribe Health News Service is a public interest newswire.

A recent survey has suggested that Americans tend to earn more money when they lose weight. While the results varied depending on race and gender, weight loss, especially weight loss that moved an individual from overweight to normal weight, resulted in a significant increase in income. The survey remains unclear on why weight loss is connected to increased wealth. It is possible that overweight individuals are discriminated against in the workplace and that women are rewarded for meeting a culturally accepted standard of attractiveness. These reasons, however, remain inconclusive.

Overweight Americans who lose a lot of weight also tend to build more wealth as they drop the pounds, according to new research.

The study found that the link between weight loss and wealth gains was particularly strong among white women. black women and white men also gained wealth as they lost weight, but not as much as did white women. The wealth of black men was basically unaffected by their weight.

There's no way to tell from the data whether losing weight was the reason for the gain in wealth, but the linkage was

definitely there, said Jay Zagorsky, author of the study and a research scientist at Ohio State University's Center for Human Resource Research.

"The typical person who loses or gains a few pounds had almost no change in wealth, but those who lost or gained large amounts of weight had a more dramatic change," Zagorsky said.

For example, white women who dropped their body mass index score (BMI)—a standard measure of obesity—by 10 points saw a wealth increase of $11,880. White men saw an increase of $12,720 for a similar drop, while black women increased wealth by $4,480. . . .

The National Longitudinal Survey of Youth

The study used data involving about 7,300 people who participated in the National Longitudinal Survey of Youth, which is funded primarily by the U.S. Bureau of Labor Statistics. The NLSY is a nationally representative survey of people nationwide conducted by Ohio State's Center for Human Resource Research.

The same people are interviewed repeatedly, giving Zagorsky the opportunity to see how the obesity levels and wealth of respondents changed over time. Zagorsky used data from 12 NLSY surveys conducted between 1985 and 2000. All the respondents were between 21 and 28 years old in 1985.

Using each respondent's height and weight figures, Zagorsky was able to calculate their BMI scores. Scores under 18.5 are considered underweight, 18.5 to 24.9 are normal, 25 to 29.9 are overweight, and 30 or higher are considered obese.

The respondents also gave information about their net worth, which included home values, cash savings, stocks, bonds, and auto values, among other assets. Outstanding debts were subtracted from that total to arrive at net worth.

Overall, the results showed that a one unit increase in a young person's BMI was associated with a $1,300 or 8 percent reduction in wealth. But the changes varied dramatically by ethnicity and gender.

Increases in BMI had no link with the wealth of black men, and were associated with small negative changes in the wealth of white men. Increases in BMI were linked to medium negative changes in wealth for black women and large negative changes for white women.

The results suggest each category of race and gender has a different ideal BMI to maximize wealth, Zagorsky said.

White women had peak net worth at the low end of the normal range (BMI 20), white males and black women reached peak net worth at the upper end of the normal range (BMI 24) and Bblack males peaked in the obese range (BMI 32).

The Weight Loss-Wealth Connection

Zagorsky emphasized that participants in this study had to lose quite a bit of weight to show strong improvements in wealth.

For example, when a typical young person decreased his or her BMI by one point, wealth increased by only $234. But when a person lost enough weight to go from the middle of the overweight category (BMI 27.5) to the middle of the normal category (BMI 21.7), wealth increased by an average of $4,085.

"If you really want to impact your wealth, you have to move from overweight or obese into the normal range," he said. "You can't just drop 5 or 10 pounds and change your wealth."

The data in this study can't tell us whether a person's wealth affects obesity, or whether obesity affects wealth. However, Zagorsky said it is more likely that weight influences wealth. An analysis of people in the study who received inheritances—suddenly increasing their wealth—showed no dramatic changes in their BMI scores in the following years. This suggests that wealth does not have a strong influence on weight.

However, if weight does affect wealth, there is also the question of how it does so. One possible explanation would be that overweight and obese people are discriminated against in the workforce, and don't earn as much money as normal weight people. Women, particularly white women, may be held to particularly high standards for beauty, which could explain why they gained more wealth compared to men as they lost more weight. But there is no way to tell for sure from this data, Zagorsky said.

Organizations to Contact

The editors have compiled the following list of organizations concerned with the issues debated in this book. The descriptions are derived from materials provided by the organizations. All have publications or information available for interested readers. The list was compiled on the date of publication of the present volume; the information provided here may change. Be aware that many organizations take several weeks or longer to respond to inquiries, so allow as much time as possible.

**American Academy of Child and
Adolescent Psychiatry (AACAP)**
3615 Wisconsin Ave. NW, Washington, DC   20016-3007
(202) 966-7300 • fax: (202) 966-2891
Web site: www.aacap.org

AACAP is a nonprofit organization dedicated to providing parents and families with information regarding developmental, behavioral, and mental disorders that affect children and adolescents. The organization provides national public information through the distribution of the newsletter *Facts for Families* and the monthly *Journal of the American Academy of Child and Adolescent Psychiatry.*

American Dietetic Association (ADA)
120 South Riverside Plaza, Suite 2000, Chicago, IL   60606
(800) 877-1600
Web site: www.eatright.org/cps/rde/xchg/ada/hs.xsl/index.html

With approximately 65,000 members, the ADA is one of the nation's largest organizations of food and nutrition professionals. The ADA was founded in 1917 by a visionary group of women. The ADA's commitment to helping people enjoy healthy lives has led the organization to concentrate on the critical health issues of obesity, aging, nutrigenetics, and integrative medicine. The ADA's publications include the *ADA Student Scoop*, an online newsletter, and the *ADA Times*, a newsletter focusing on hot topics in nutrition.

American Psychiatric Association (APA)
1000 Wilson Blvd., Suite 1825, Arlington, VA   22209-3901
(703) 907-7300
e-mail: apa@psych.org
Web site: www.psych.org

APA is an organization of psychiatrists dedicated to studying the nature, treatment, and prevention of mental disorders. It helps create mental health policies, distributes information about psychiatry, and promotes psychiatric research and education. APA publishes the monthly *American Journal of Psychiatry*.

American Psychological Association
750 First St. NE, Washington, DC   20002-4242
(202) 336-5500 • fax: (202) 336-5708
e-mail: public.affairs@apa.org
Web site: www.apa.org

This society of psychologists aims to "advance psychology as a science, as a profession, and as a means of promoting human welfare." It produces numerous publications, including the monthly journal *American Psychologist*, the monthly newspaper *APA Monitor*, and the quarterly *Journal of Abnormal Psychology*.

Anorexia Nervosa and Bulimia Association (ANAB)
767 Bayridge Dr., PO Box 20058, Kingston, ON
  K7P 1CO
  Canada
Web site: www.phe.queensu.ca/anab/index.html

ANAB is a nonprofit organization of health professionals, volunteers, and past and present victims of eating disorders and their families and friends. The organization advocates and coordinates support for individuals affected directly or indirectly by eating disorders. As part of its effort to offer a broad range of current information, opinion, and/or advice concerning eating disorders, body image, and related issues, ANAB produces the quarterly newsletter *Reflections*.

**Anorexia Nervosa and Related
Eating Disorders, Inc. (ANRED)**
PO Box 5102, Eugene, OR   97405
(503) 344-1144
Web site: www.anred.com

ANRED is a nonprofit organization that provides information about anorexia nervosa, bulimia nervosa, binge-eating disorder, compulsive exercising, and other lesser-known food and weight disorders, including details about recovery and prevention. ANRED offers workshops, individual and professional training, as well as local community education. It also produces a monthly newsletter.

Health Canada
Tower A, Qualicum Towers, 2936 Baseline Road,
3rd Floor, A.L. 3303D
Ottawa, ON   K1A OK9
   Canada
(866) 225-0709
Web site: www.hc-sc.gc.ca/index_e.html

Health Canada is the federal department responsible for helping Canadians maintain and improve their health. Health Canada relies on high-quality scientific research and conducts ongoing consultations with Canadians to determine long-term health care needs. Health Canada encourages Canadians to take an active role in their heath and issues publications, including *Canada's Food Guide to Healthy Eating*.

Healthy Refrigerator
5775-G Peachtree-Dunwoody Rd., Suite 500
Atlanta, GA   30342

(404) 252-3663
Web site: www.healthyfridge.org

The Healthy Refrigerator includes nutrition and health recommendations for children and adults along with recipes, articles, and quizzes. A "Just For Kids" section offers facts about heart disease and a "healthy fridge" quiz.

Juvenile Diabetes Research
Foundation International (JDRFI)
120 Wall St., New York, NY   10005-4001
(800) 533-CURE
Web site: www.jdrf.org

JDRF is the leading charitable organization and advocate of type 1 (juvenile) diabetes research worldwide. The mission of JDRF is to find a cure for diabetes and its complications through the support of research. JDRF publishes *Countdown Magazine, Countdown For Kids,* and *Life With Diabetes,* an e-newsletter.

KidsHealth.org
P.O. Box 269, Wilmington, DE   19899
Web site: www.kidshealth.org/kid

KidsHealth is a Web site providing doctor-approved health information about children from before birth through adolescence. Created by the Nemours Foundation's Center for Children's Health Media, KidsHealth provides families with accurate, up-to-date, and jargon-free health information they can use. KidsHealth has been on the Web since 1995.

Mayo Health Clinic
200 First St. SW, Rochester, MN   55905
(507) 284-2511
Web site: www.mayoclinic.com

The Mayo Clinic is a not-for-profit medical practice devoted to the diagnosis and treatment of virtually every type of complex illness. Doctors, specialists, and other health care professionals provide comprehensive diagnoses, understandable answers, and effective treatment. The Mayo Clinic has sites in Rochester, Minnesota, Jacksonville, Florida, and Scottsdale-Phoenix, Arizona. Collectively, the three locations treat more than half a million people each year.

National Association of Anorexia and Associated Disorders (ANAD)
Box 7, Highland Park, IL   60035
(847) 831-3438 • fax: (847) 433-4632
e-mail: anad20@aol.com
Web site: http://members.aol.com/anad20

ANAD offers hot-line counseling, operates an international network of support groups for people with eating disorders and their families, and provides referrals to health care professionals who treat eating disorders. It produces a quarterly newsletter and information packets and organizes national conferences and local programs. All ANAD services are provided free of charge.

Society for Adolescent Medicine (SAM)
1916 NW Copper Oaks Circle, Blue Springs, MO   64015
(816) 224-8010
Web site: www.adolescenthealth.org

SAM is a multidisciplinary organization of professionals committed to improving the physical and psychosocial health and well-being of all adolescents. It helps plan and coordinate national and international professional education programs on adolescent health. Its publications include the monthly *Journal of Adolescent Health* and the quarterly *SAM Newsletter*.

Something Fishy
PO Box 837, Holbrook, NY   11741
(866) 690-7239
Web site: www.something-fishy.org

Something Fishy is dedicated to raising awareness and emphasizing that eating disorders are neither about food nor weight. Eating disorders, the organization maintains, are just the symptoms of something deeper going on inside. Something Fishy is determined to remind each and every eating disorder sufferer that he or she is not alone, and that complete recovery is possible.

United States Department of Agriculture (USDA)
1400 Independence Ave. SW, Washington, DC   20250
(202) 720-2791
Web site: www.usda.gov/wps/portal/usdahome

The USDA promotes U.S. agricultural products and provides information pertaining to nutrition, obesity prevention, meal planning, and food labels. The USDA Web site also includes multiple food pyramids designed to outline the nutrition needs of various age groups. The USDA issues a weekly newsletter, *Broadcaster's Letter*, and publishes the *Agricultural Fact Book* annually.

Bibliography

Books

Ray Audette, Troy Gilchrist, Raymond V. Audette, and Michael R. Eades	*Neanderthin: Eat Like a Caveman to Achieve a Lean, Strong, Healthy Body.* New York: St. Martin's Paperbacks, 2000.
Carol Beck	*Nourishing Your Daughter: Help Your Child Develop a Heathy Relationship with Food and Her Body.* New York: Perigee, 2001.
Debbie Danowski and Pedro Lazaro	*Why Can't I Stop Eating?: Recognizing, Understanding, and Overcoming Food Addiction.* Center City, MN: Hazelden, 2000.
Marilyn Glenville	*Natural Alternatives to Dieting.* London: Kyle Cathie Limited, reprint edition, 2003.
Donald Hensrud, ed.	*Mayo Clinic Healthy Weight for Everybody.* New York: Mayo Clinic, reissue edition, 2005.
Miriam Hoffer	*Fuelling Body, Mind and Spirit: A Balanced Approach to Healthy Eating.* Toronto: Sumach Press, 2000.
Carol Johnson and Gary D. Foster	*Self-Esteem Comes in All Sizes: How to Be Happy and Healthy at Your Natural Weight.* Carlsbad, CA: Gurze Books, revised edition, 2001.

Ronni Litz Julien   *What Should I Feed My Kids? How to Keep Your Children Healthy by Teaching Them to Eat Right.* Franklin Lake, NJ: New Page Books, 2006.

Joanne Kimes   *Dieting Sucks: What to Do When Your Waistline Makes You Miserable.* Cincinnati, OH: Adams Media Corporation, 2006.

Daniel S. Kirschenbaum   *The Healthy Obsession Program: Smart Weight Loss Instead of Low-Carb Lunacy.* Dallas, TX: Benbella Books, 2006.

Deborah M. Michel and Susan G. Willard   *When Dieting Becomes Dangerous: A Guide to Understanding and Treating Anorexia and Bulimia.* New Haven, CT: Yale University Press, 2002.

Dianne Neumark-Sztainer   *"I'm, Like, SO Fat!" Helping Your Teen Make Healthy Choices About Eating and Exercise in a Weight-Obsessed World.* New York: Guilford, 2005.

Jane Ogden   *The Psychology of Eating: From Healthy to Disordered Behavior.* Malden, MA: Blackwell Publishing, 2002.

Jamie Pope and Martin Katahn   *The Low Fat Supermarket Shopper's Guide, Revised and Updated Edition: Making Healthy Choices from Thousands of Brand Name Foods.* New York: W. W. Norton, 2005.

Sally Robinson   *Healthy Eating in Primary Schools.*
London: Paul Chapman Educational
Publishing, 2006.

Bob Schwartz   *Diets Don't Work: Stop Dieting Be-*
come Naturally Thin Live a Diet-Free
Life. Houston, TX: Breakthru Publishing, third edition, 2005.

Walter Willett   *Eat, Drink, and Be Healthy: The Har-*
and P.J. Skerrett   *vard Medical School Guide to Heathy*
Eating. New York: Free Press, 2005.

Periodicals

Martha Barnette   "Why Diets Are Dumb," *Glamour,*
December 2005.

Caroline Bollinger   "The Diet Docs' Crash Diets," *Preven-*
tion, September 2006.

Amby Burfoot   "Should You Be on a Diet?" *Runner's*
World, November 2004.

Better Nutrition   "Can You Really 'Cheat' on a Diet
and Still Lose Weight?" November
2003.

Cathy R. Cohen   "Dieting Dilemma: Does Anything
Really Work?" *Westchester County*
Business Journal, April 26, 2004.

Stacey Colino   "Can You Undo Your Past Health
Mistakes?" *Redbook,* July 2005.

Daryn Eller   "Read This Before You Start Any
Diet," *Prevention,* January 2005.

Joel Fuhrman and Jeff Novick — "Atkins & South Beach Diets," *Health Science*, Fall 2004.

Beatrice Trum Hunter — "Déjà Vu ... All Over Again," *Consumers' Research Magazine*, April 2003.

David L. Katz — "The Way to Eat," *O, The Oprah Magazine*, December 2006.

Kristen Kemp — "The Don't-You-Dare-Diet Diet," *Girls' Life*, February–March 2006.

Good Housekeeping — "Our Eat-Smart Diet Plan," October 2006.

Consumer Reports — "Rating the Diets from Atkins to Dr. Sears' Zone," June 2005.

Geneen Roth — "My Diet Moment of Truth: What Really Got My Attention and Made Me Drop My Bad Habits," *Prevention*, June 2005.

Francine Russo — "Your Mirror Image?" *Time*, June 6, 2005.

Helen Truby — "Clinical Viewpoint—Are Commercial Diets Useful?" *GP*, September 1, 2006.

Economist (US) — "We Are What We Eat," September 6, 2003.

Newsweek — "Weighing the Medical Evidence: How Can We Lose Weight? Protect Our Hearts? Control Blood Pressure? Docs Are Divided," December 8, 2003.

Current Health 2, A Weekly Reader Publication "What You Need to Know About Fad Diets," September 2003.

Index